MW01077505

The Narcissist Survival Guide

Everything you need to know to deal with

the

Narcissists in your world,

... without losing your mind.

BY WENDY POWELL

Acknowledgements

I want to thank all of the individuals who have shared their stories with me. A special thanks goes to Jan Sherman who has a great eye for detail and helped me clean up the first version. I would like to make a special mention of Jaucelynn who edited some pretty raw writing and my other daughters that supported me through this process. I'm sure it hasn't been easy listening to me talking about the same subject, for an eternity, but your attention allowed me to flesh out my observations and draw my conclusions. It is greatly appreciated.

This is book is dedicated
to all of those individuals
who have struggled through
a relationship with
a
narcissist.

Visit the author's website at: www.wendypowell.ca

The Narcissist Survival Guide

Author's Notes

Honesty, integrity and love are at the very foundation of our civilization. Our ability to come together, live in communities and find synergies from working in groups has allowed us to dominate this planet as a species and raise our standard of living beyond what was believable, even a century ago. If we were unable to trust one another, we would not be able to avail ourselves to the benefits of society because we would be forever fearful that someone would exploit us. Narcissists do not share this point of view. They believe that the entire world is there to meet their needs. Honesty, integrity and love do not curtail their activities.

For the first few decades of my life, the diagnosis of Narcissistic Personality Disorder (NPD) did not exist. That does not mean that narcissists themselves did not exist and let me assure you that they did. My writing is based on my personal experience, patterns I've seen while coaching clients that are dealing with a narcissist and reading books and blogs on the topic.

My title is doctor, but that refers to a veterinary degree and should not be confused with a human medical doctor or a Ph.D. in psychology or psychiatry. In short, this book reflects my opinions and my experiences and should not be seen as a replacement for professional guidance on this topic.

My hope is that through this book more people will come to understand this pathology and learn how to recognize it in others and protect themselves from it, as much as possible. Once you know you are dealing with a narcissist it greatly reduces the power that they have over you.

Best of luck,

Wendy

Author's Notes on Version 3

In many ways the writing of this book was a coming of age for me. I had attained a certain level of understanding of pathological narcissism, enough to write a small "guide" and so I set out to pull the info all into one spot.

When together, the holes between the knowledgeable bits were blatant. So, I went on a journey of discovery to fill in the gaps in my understanding.

I hit a major bump when I realized that my mother was a narcissist, and I had to reevaluate all of what I knew of my childhood. Fun stuff. This knowledge lead to more insight into why I had come to where I am in my understanding of narcissism, but that's a different book.

So the book needed to go through a second revision as my research branched into areas that I had not anticipated. This time, I'm promising myself that this version, my third, will be the last on this particular book. If I understand more in the future, I'll just have to set off and write another book.

The beauty of course, of electronic publishing, is that these changes are very easy to do. Not so for the hard copy, unfortunately. But, at some point one must finish and consider a project complete. So I am done.

Introduction

The word narcissism is being bandied about like a trend right now and it is getting confusing for those of us who actually have a pathological narcissist in our lives. Narcissism is not just another word for arrogant or conceited. You are not a narcissist because you post a lot of things on the web or take a lot of 'selfies'. Narcissism, in the psychological sense of the word is a pathology, a dangerous pathology.

Pure and simple, it is the inability to be empathetic, to know or care how other's feel.

These behavioural traits have become insidious in our society because so many of them are becoming admired from the perspective of the "dog eat dog" mentality. Discussions occur asking whether or not the head of a company "should" be a narcissist, which means that when it comes to being successful, the ability to overlook the pain you cause others -- is somehow acceptable. Lying for sex, wink, wink, is another example of non-caring behaviour that got more acceptance than it ever should have.

Accurately or not, many successful people have been described as narcissists and in societies largely ruled by the pursuit of money, their actions become acceptable. The war cry, that the ends justify the means comes down to the personal level, the level of the kitchen.

The best place to start is learning how to identify the true narcissists in your life. I start Part 1 by explaining how to spot them and I go into more depth about the way that the diagnosis is actually made. In Part 2 I move into the nuts and bolts of dealing with them, regardless of your relationship. Then we come to Part 3 the hard bit. This is an opportunity to examine yourself and understand the possible impact a narcissist has had on who you are and how you see the world.

Part 1: Are They A Narcissist?

Lack of empathy is the gold standard test for pathological narcissism (NPD) but it is difficult to know what that looks like. I will describe the traits many narcissists have and give the medical definition. This is the technical description of what narcissism is.

Then I get more personal and show examples of how these people look in real life, while dating them and if they are part of your work space or family. I'd also like to introduce three fictional characters. Bob, Dave and Susan. These are caricatures that help me explain an oversimplified stereotype of typical narcissist. No one is going to be exactly like any of these three, but it will give you a better idea of how "everyday" some of their behaviours can seem.

Bob always has to be the centre of attention and needs multiple people around all of the time to feed his desire for adoration. Generally, people either really like him or really dislike him, but for the most part, he is just thought of as arrogant and full of himself. The people in his life who only know him casually think he is just a bit of a jerk. It is only those that know him well that realize how deep the pathology goes. He is usually reading a newspaper, or preoccupied with something and it is not obvious that he has a need to always be actively stimulated all of the time.

Dave, on the other hand, is quiet and could be considered introverted. He still thinks that he is the only one that has any importance and he is incapable of caring if he hurts other people. No one has ever accused him of being arrogant, much less a narcissist, but he is still callous and uncaring and does not see the importance of others. Dave uses withdrawal and the silent treatment to shift the power to himself. He is the guy that forgets to call and doesn't follow through on plans and promises. When called out for this behaviour, he quickly deflects the fault to you.

Susan has been using her sex appeal to manipulate the men in her life since she can remember. As a narcissist, she looks down on others and has realized that flaunting her sexuality gets her what she wants. Many narcissists use sex as a weapon, but there is a difference between the sexes on how this plays out. If you don't have anything to offer her, she will just pass over you or ignore you completely. Her one child is both an inconvenience and a star, depending on Susan's mood.

By the end of this part you should know what to look for if you suspect a narcissist in your life. You should also be able to begin to see how unacceptable some of the behaviours that are condoned by our society actually are.

Narcissism Defined

The DSM (*Diagnostic and Statistical Manual of Mental Disorders*), published by the American Psychiatric Association, outlines the basis for the diagnosis of mental disorders. It defines Narcissistic Personality Disorder (NPD) as:

"A pervasive pattern of grandiosity (in fantasy or behavior), need for admiration, and lack of empathy, beginning by early adulthood and present in a variety of contexts, as indicated by five (or more) of the following:

1. has a grandiose sense of self-importance (e.g., exaggerates achievements and talents, expects to be recognized as superior without commensurate achievements)

2. is preoccupied with fantasies of unlimited success, power, brilliance, beauty, or ideal love

3. believes that he or she is "special" and unique and can only be understood by, or should associate with, other special or high-status people (or institutions)

4. requires excessive admiration

5. has a sense of entitlement, i.e., takes advantage of others to achieve his or her own ends

6. lacks empathy: is unwilling to recognize or identify with the feelings and needs of others

7. is often envious of others or believes that others are envious of him or her

8. shows arrogant, haughty behaviors or attitudes" [1]

On a more day-to-day basis, the narcissist stands out because of the way they behave and how they treat other people. Depending on the relationship that you have with the narcissist, and I go into more detail in later chapters, you may or may not see the traits that will let you know you are dealing with one.

For instance, narcissists need constant *nourishment* from others, so they do not want to be alone. This may not be obvious if they are a co-worker or a neighbour because quite frankly, you have no idea what they are doing most of the time. If, however, you live with them, you will know they are almost always 'with' someone. Bob, for instance, may need to chat on a computer or have a phone conversation even is someone is home. A warm body is not enough; he needs to actually be engaged with the person. So, if you are with a narcissist, but are busy, they will find someone else to speak to.

Sue has many lovers and when her husband is at work, she goes out to find companionship. All of her lovers are confused about the status of the relationship and she has become more careful about arguing with them and "breaking-up" so that they can't expect as much from her between each dalliance.

Dave has multiple friends and is known to just sit in his car and phone people until he finds someone that is available. This gives him a "spontaneous" appearance and people like how fluid his life appears to be.

Nourishment

Required constantly by a narcissist. This is adoration, hero-worshiping, love, sex and compliments that come from the people in their lives who think that they are wonderful. Narcissists need a **constant supply of nourishment** *and will have many people in their lives to provide it.*

Narcissists view all of the people they include in their lives as 'inferior', which seems to be in conflict with number 3 of the DSM definition, above, but isn't actually. They will let you know you are not as important as the people they normally spend their time with. It makes them feel superior to surround themselves with people they can look down on.

The people they have in their lives always serve them. Bob loves admirers and Sue wants sex partners. Dave is happy with anyone that he can hang out with, especially if he can entertain himself by creating havoc in their lives. So anyone that they consider a friend is someone who can provide them with something. Be it admiration, sex, entertainment, money, opportunity, support, or simply someone willing to do the day to day work of living like shopping and cleaning.

They usually need to be 'preoccupied' with something. This takes the form of always amusing themselves. It is not enough for them to be content for a moment. This necessitates Dave sitting in his car phoning people for companionship. He cannot be bored. Far be it for narcissists to stop and admire a full moon, for instance. An extended moment like that does nothing for them and they are more likely to say, "I've seen it." In a way that lets you know that stopping to enjoy this sight is beneath them, but really, they have to be kept entertained, actively occupied, and viewing beauty, for any length of time, does not cut it.

Great amounts of energy, thought and time are spent on revenge schemes. Narcissists usually have one or more *receptacles* for their hate and anger. When Bob hates, he hates completely. Those that have "wronged" him will be criticized at every opportunity and to every audience. It is important for him to ceaselessly try to discredit this individual, even to people that barely know him.

But, it is not enough to despise these people from afar, narcissist spend a lot of thought on making the lives of people they target a living hell. In closer relationships this can take the form of picking fights and being purposefully mean, but in more casual relationships, the narcissist is more likely to spread rumours, sabotage or annoy their receptacles.

> ## *Receptacle*
>
> *Required by a narcissist. One or more people are required to be the focus of the narcissist's anger. This person or people will be the focus of elaborate and unrelenting revenge scenarios.*

A serious sign that someone is a narcissist is they can lie easily, devoid of all the normal nervousness. Bob, Sue and Dave are equally adept at this. It does not matter what type of a relationship you have with a narcissist, they will lie to you. These are not the normal social lies that skew the evidence slightly to make one look better or the niceties like, "Your new hair cut looks great on you!" These are boldface lies or deletions of great pieces of information that give a totally different meaning to the story. A favourite example of such a lie is describing a public hanging as: while on stage at a public event, a platform gave way and he died in the fall. Dissembling is their thing.

An interesting point that might not be obvious unless your relationship is quite personal like a lover, sibling, or family member, is that they will lie about things for no apparent reason. I believe this is a way of making themselves feel superior. They may think, "If you are stupid enough to believe this lie, then you deserve to be lied to."

In close relationships this might leave you feeling like you are forgetful, losing your mind or confused. It is a form of amusement for them and is best illustrated in the 1938 stage play, "Gas Light". In this story the husband tries to convince his wife and others that she is insane by turning the gas up and down, making the lighting shift, among other things. It is direct manipulation to make her look and feel insane. She may have crossed him at some point and he is trying to get revenge. This is an example of a receptacle.

At work a narcissist can be described as a person who never takes responsibility for anything. Everything that goes wrong is someone else's fault. Dave ensures that everyone in his office knows that his co-worker is incompetent. If something goes wrong he is quick to implicate this particular co-worker. Narcissists usually have one or several enemies, or receptacles, they blame for their problems. They are key perpetrators of using people against one another and creating drama in order to take the focus off themselves.

Their inability to form normal emotional attachments with people plays out in very dangerous ways. Sue's multiple sexual partners puts all of them at risk if an infection is introduced to this mix. They don't care what happens to other people, whether or not the other people are hurt or how their behaviours affect those around them. Simply described above as, "lacks empathy" actually means they will hurt you without caring. This can be seen in their callous nature, never taking responsibility for things, lying, manipulating and creating drama.

In order to receive the adoration that nourishes them, narcissists must never get angry with most of the people they deal with. These relationships are based on lies that allow the other person to like or admire the narcissist and often the narcissist feels contempt for the person who 'believes' them and therefore must be very stupid (in the eyes of the narcissist). It is not surprising that a lot of rage builds up inside of the narcissist. In order to release this anger the narcissist causes conflict in personal relationships and often has one or more "receptacles" for these negative emotions. This receptacle will get picked on and bullied by the narcissist.

Entire families might join the narcissist and make one child in the family the receptacle, or in this case, the scapegoat for all of the family's problems.

This type of conflict shows in every aspect of who they are and anyone that constantly seems to be in a battle with other people is likely the source of the problem, even if they are only in battle with one person -- as far as you are aware. Normal people get angry with someone and then let it go after a while. The narcissist is out to discredit this person and will continually mention how bad they are and the awful things that they have done. This puts the narcissist in the position of not taking responsibility for things (because they can blame the receptacle) and they can take on the victim stance because this other person does so many bad things to them (whether these things are true or not).

Finally, many narcissists play the victim role. It could be that their parents, friends, lovers, bosses or whomever, have mistreated them. They have been the victims. This, of course, fits into the web of lying, wanting to be the centre of attention, creating drama, not taking responsibility for things and needing to have someone with them all of the time. Convincing someone to feel sorry for you is a sure way to get them to take care of you, at least for now...

The confusing thing about narcissists is that they can be kind and thoughtful, especially when they want something. Some narcissists can be very charismatic and lets not forget the sex appeal inherent in a promiscuous person. They are not encumbered by having to tell the truth, so they freely tell you want you want to hear. They believe they are the only one who matters, so they are not concerned if they hurt you, or deceive you, if they get what they want. One way to do that is to convince you that you like them. This means that many of us can become involved in a relationship that we initially think is with a kind, thoughtful, charismatic person, until the truth surfaces...

1. Michael B. First, Allen Frances, Harold Alan Pincus, *DSM-IV-TR guidebook* (Arlington, VA: American Psychiatric Publishing, Inc., 2004) 364-365. http://ow.ly/28l81x

The Top 20 Traits of a Narcissist

Let's put this into point form so that it is easier to reference. The way the traits are experienced vary with the type of relationship that you have, and it can be very different for the various situations, so I have gone into more detail in the following chapters.

I am talking specifically about Narcissistic Personality Disorder (NPD). It is not important if the person is just a liar or just arrogant. The reason NPD individuals are more important is that they can be very dangerous. They do not care about the consequences of their actions or whether or not anyone is hurt, so they are not only unpleasant but a threat to your safety and emotional well-being.

Here is a list of the Top 20 Traits that most narcissists have. Not all narcissists have all of the traits. It is easy to remember how narcissists behave because all relationships must serve them and they must feel superior to everyone. They want you to be their SLAVE, so let's use it as an acronym.

Top 20 Traits of a Narcissist

Superior
Liars
Attack
Victims
Emotions

Superior

1. They must always feel superior and they like to talk about how great they are. This includes always needing to be right and to win at all costs. They take satisfaction in the failings of others.

2. They do not acknowledge the accomplishments of others and they treat the people around them as inferior, often by lying to them and deceiving them.

3. They are very demanding and expect people to serve them. All of their friendships are with people they feel superior to (younger, less educated, less accomplished) and are based on what the individual can do for them. The narcissist needs to be nourished with praise from many people.

4. They like to brag about outrageous and dangerous things that they have done which can make them seem exciting and "better" than everyone else.

Liars

5. They lie for any or no reason or to manipulate or confuse you.

6. They are unreliable, don't take responsibility for things and will blame other people if something goes wrong.

7. They are charming, charismatic and solicitous when they want to be, but this is just an act and is very dishonest.

Attack

8. They are promiscuous and use sex as a weapon.

9. They do not understand boundaries and will invade your privacy and personal space.

10. They will share confidences with others as a way of undermining you.

11. They are quick to anger and their mood can shift unpredictably.

12. They will use physical intimidation and violence to control.

13. They will use public humiliation to keep you insecure and they think nothing of yelling at people, including sales people, servers or others that they feel are beneath them.

Victims

14. They have a history of bad relationships usually involving a lot of drama.

15. They see themselves as the victim and will try to elicit sympathy.

Emotions

16. They determine which emotions are acceptable and criticize anyone that expresses other emotions.

17. They show no consideration for people in pain and will belittle others for being too soft, generous or trusting.

18. Love is always conditional. They give love in exchange for you giving them something.

19. They will manipulate you using your emotions and human needs against you.

20. They hate to be alone and must always be busy.

Signs that You are Dating a Narcissist

I hate to freak you out, but if you have found yourself with a sibling, parent or lover that is a narcissist, there is a better chance that the next person you get close to will be a narcissist as well. Whether we like it or not, we find their behaviours familiar, we understand them, and it puts us at risk immediately. "Us" being those of us that have loved a narcissist before.

The ability to recognize a narcissist is a very valuable tool. It is often difficult to know at the beginning of a relationship because we are still trying to figure out who this person is. Add in the fact that it is always exciting to meet someone new and we are all hopeful this person will turn out to be someone who we can stay with and you have a recipe for disaster. Here are some red flags that should make you question whether or not you are with a narcissist.

1. They are VERY interested in you.

When you first meet, your initial conversations have less of a 'get to know you' feel and are more like an interrogation. They may join in the conversation, but they tend to want to know as much about you as possible. They ask a lot of questions, want to know about what is important to you, what your other relationships are like and how your last romantic relationship ended. This may make you feel slightly uncomfortable because the questions they ask can be quite personal very early in the relationship. This is the initial situation, soon they become very full of themselves and only want to talk about how great they are.

Why this pulls you in:

They show so much interest in you when you first meet them. This can be irresistible to someone who has been ignored, unheard or otherwise lonely. This burst of attention can make you feel like this person cares about you. If you desperately want some attention, you are at risk. Also, there is an illusion that you are really getting to know this person. They appear open and willing to discuss painful and unpleasant things right away.

2. They reveal something very personal early.

Most people share private details with someone as they get to know them. In a relationship with a narcissist it is different, because these personal details are shared long before the relationship warrants this type of exchange. Bob is quick to tell you about his brush with the law. Others might try to hide this, but Bob has learned that it makes him appears interesting and somewhat of a victim. Sue drops in a comment about a preferred fetish and pretends to act shy about it.

These topics may come up when they are asking you questions, as discussed above, because they are trying to learn private things about you. They may share a 'personal' thing about themselves that gives the illusion of them opening up to you. It is likely something that is well known to everyone, but you don't know that.

Why this pulls you in:

Revealing something personal is associated with attaining a certain level of intimacy. This is often reciprocated.

Rule of Thumb for Personal Information

If you wouldn't feel comfortable with everyone at work knowing something about you, it is not something to share in the first couple of weeks of a relationship.

In normal social interactions, people want the same level of vulnerability. We all want close, personal, relationships. When they tell you something personal, there is an overwhelming desire to share something with them to show that you want to be that close.

Sharing personal things before you have known someone very long (regardless of how close you feel!!) is risky because they can and will use this personal information against you.

3. They elicit sympathy.

They give you a reason to feel sorry for them: broken home, lost job, just got out of a bad relationship, hard times. This is another emotional ploy. It is instinctive to pick up a small bird that has fallen out of a tree and try to nurse it back to health. They know this. It has worked before. If you bite, they have you.

Why this pulls you in:

This plays on our natural instincts to help one another. If someone shows vulnerability we want to help. One of the most common examples is that their last lover was very mean to them and treated them badly. They now are hurt, vulnerable and scared to get involved with another person. We can all relate to having an Ex that hurt us. This helps build the relationship by creating a common experience, a common understanding. If you did have a bad relationship before, they find this alluring. They want drama in their lives and if you get pulled into Ex bashing, they have found a true partner.

4. All of their spare time must be with you.

Narcissists cannot be alone. Do not mistake this for them really, really wanting to spend time with you. They are trying to avoid being alone. They have a need that has to be met and they want to know right away if you are going to meet that need for them. They say that they like your company and want to be with you when in fact they are separating you from your friends, your hobbies and your family, which ultimately makes them very powerful in your life because there is no one else.

Why this pulls you in:

If you have been lonely, or alone too much, this can make you feel special and loved.

5. Quickly, they start making long-term plans.

They can see your future for decades. They get really close really fast, well before it would normally happen. They have this idealized dream of everlasting true love and convince you that you are the centerpiece.

Why this pulls you in:

They want you to see this imaginary future and start making long-term plans. Later, this will be used against you if you try to break away from the relationship because this imaginary life is something that you have agreed to and probably want. This is the opposite of someone who "won't commit" and can be misunderstood as desirable. It is actually a ploy to keep you locked in the relationship when things start to fall apart.

6. They display anger disproportionate to the situation.

Anyone that has road rage, gets snippy with a clerk, waiter or someone they barely have contact with is showing inappropriate anger. It can be subtle at the time, but is MAJOR. Normal people do not have this amount of pent up rage. This demonstrates a complete lack of consideration for the other person and you need to know that this will be directed at you in time.

Why this pull you in:

If you tend to lack assertiveness, it can be nice to be with someone who stands up for you. It can also make you feel like they are coming to your defense and that they have your back.

7. They blame others for all of their problems.

They do not take responsibility for the loss of their last relationship, job, friends, or anything else. If they sound reasonable and can explain why each relationship failed and why it was not their fault, you may believe them.

Why this pulls you in:

It can give you a misrepresentation of who they are and not let you see how much trouble they cause. It also elicits sympathy because they have had such a hard time. It has a secondary effect of allowing them to appear gracious. Saying things like, "we grew apart", sounds so evolved when in fact the last lover had to get a restraining order.

8. They have a need to know where you are and whom you are with at all times.

They blame this on their last relationship and make you feel like it is up to you to make them feel safe and loved, because they were hurt so bad before. These are actually check-up calls so that they can keep track of you. Also, constant interruptions from this person while you are with others can lead to disturbances in your existing relationships.

Why this pulls you in:

It can make you feel special and loved to have someone contacting you to say hello. These calls (texts, emails or whatever) are often masked as, "I miss you and wanted to say hello."

9. They lie.

They exaggerate or give only partial information about things. For example, their last job may have been lost because they didn't show up for work. They say that their boss was a jerk. Dave suggests that he outshined his superior at work, so his boss got him fired. They say things that make them appear better than they are, more like the person you want them to be.

Why this pulls you in:

They are pulling on your heartstrings by telling lies that inflate them, make them look like the victim or make them seem interesting. They may simply be telling you that they are who you want them to be. Many people in relationships with narcissists believe they have found their soul mate because the narcissist just described themselves as the exact person they wanted. For instance, they may exaggerate how close they are to their parents if they know that family is important to you.

10. History of reckless behaviour.

They tell stories about great and daring things they have done. If you listen carefully, many of these activities are actually dangerous and stupid. It might sound thrilling, but many narcissists will do things that normal people would consider too risky.

Why this pulls you in:

These stories are often interesting and make the person seem daring and exciting. It feels like being with them will make your life more expansive and enjoyable. If you have been shy or conservative in your approach to life, thinking you are with someone who will expand your horizons and introduce you to new adventures can sound exciting.

Discouraging a Narcissist

Armed with the knowledge that we might be dating a narcissist, there are some things that can help you dissuade them before you know whether or not they are trouble. So, let's turn the above information around and see how we "should" behave in a new relationship and I'll do my best to explain why this would scare a narcissist away.

1. In initial conversations make sure you ask them as many questions as they ask you.

Wait for an answer. If they say that they like something, ask a more specific question.

Why this is important

Narcissists actually probe you for information so that they can learn as much about you as possible. By asking them questions, you force them to tell you about themselves. This slows down the process of them collecting data and allows you an opportunity to determine if they are lying.

For example, you say, "I love dancing the Macarena" They reply, "I do too!" You can ask, "Where do you usually go dancing?" This next direct question forces them to be more specific. The first set of lies is very simple, but the more detailed the questions the more likely you will catch them in a lie. Also, it can put them off balance and make them less attracted to you.

It is important in any relationship
that there be reciprocity,
so asking someone about themselves
as much as they ask you,
is a good thing.

2. Never reveal private information early.

> ## *Rule of Thumb for Personal Information*
>
> *If you wouldn't feel comfortable with everyone at work knowing something about you, it is not something to share in the first couple of weeks of a relationship.*

Why this is important

Sharing personal information has two effects. The first is that it gives you a sense of intimacy with this person. Exchanging private information is one of the ways that we get close to someone. Narcissists use this method to get close fast. Getting really close to someone before you know them is never a good thing.

The second problem is that sensitive material can be used against you and if the person turns out to be a narcissist you will regret sharing things that you did not want everyone to know.

Realize we all crave intimacy.
There is a strong urge to reveal things to the same level as someone else.

It is good to base any relationship on trust and intimacy and these things take time. There will be time in the future to share these details if this is the right person.

3. Resist the urge to "take care of someone" you just met.

If someone tells you early in a relationship that they have come upon bad times at work, in health, a tragedy, ask yourself why you want to take care of them and why there is no one else in their lives to fulfill this role.

Why this is important

This is one of the tactics that narcissists use to get close to you. Examples are, "I've just lost my job and have no money". "I was living with my last lover and I ended it, so I have no place to live". "I just moved into town and have been living on a friend's sofa but I've outstayed my welcome". If they say that they just got out of a bad relationship with an awful person, insist that you don't want to be their rebound person and move away quickly.

Realize that you are fighting instincts here.
We all want to pick up the fallen bird and nurse it back to
health.

Healthy relationships are between two
self-sufficient individuals.
If this person cannot support themselves now,
they are unlikely to take care of
their half of the responsibility in a relationship.

4. Maintain your private time.

If you are being flooded with attention it may initially feel like you are loved. This is not the case. A narcissist will flood you with attention as a way of controlling you. You get used to this level of attention and then you expect it, long after it is taken away. Try to not respond to the multiple texts, messages and calls. Don't respond until it is convenient. Constantly interrupting your time with other people is one of the ways that narcissists distance you from your friends.

Why this is important

Narcissists need constant nourishment from others. They are trying to figure out if you are the one that is going to give it to them. By not giving it to them, you are less likely to be pursued.

A person that actually loves you, respects your right to privacy, time with your friends and your need to have time to yourself.

5. We all like to dream and plan, but the beginning of a relationship is a bad time to be planning to be together forever.

Try the phrase, "I think we are getting ahead of ourselves". This allows you to be honest and can be used like this: "Yes, I would love to move to New York City with you and pursue my comedy career, but I think we are getting ahead of ourselves."

Why this is important

One of the tactics narcissists use to keep you from leaving is to point out that you "agreed" to this relationship and wanted this relationship from the beginning. Now you are a "quitter" or "selfish" or "mean" if you are just abandoning this dream. Often, the dream was premature.

**It is good to have dreams and long term plans
but these should be based on a solid relationship,
not an elusive goal,
that is agreed upon before all of the facts are in.**

6. Pay attention to how they treat others.

Ask yourself if you want to be treated that way.

Why this is important

Narcissists often think that they are justified belittling those around them. They think that they are superior and therefore they can treat others badly. In any relationship, how your partner treats others can be how they will treat you -- eventually.

A nice person has respect for others and respect for you and treats people accordingly.

7. Don't fight for the relationship right at the beginning.

If someone that you are just starting to date tells you that their friends or family would not approve of your relationship or if they let you know that they are leaving town or that they are worried about you breaking up with them right away it is a warning sign.

They are looking for assurances, way before it is reasonable, for you to say that you would not leave. If for any reason, the relationship seems to have opposition or an expiry date, see it as a red flag. Statements like, "This is just a summer fling" are warning signs.

Why this is important

Think of dating a narcissist as a job interview. They want someone that will be there for the long haul. They want to know that you will go the extra mile to make the relationship work. All of these things are desirable in a good, long-term relationship, but they show you are desperate in the short term. Narcissists are attracted to someone that is too desperate to easily leave any relationship, even a bad one.

If their friends or family wouldn't approve, why would you want to be with someone when you would be an outcast or disliked?

If the person you just started dating may have to leave town for a job or to go back to school, recognize that it is too early to make that kind of commitment and don't. These situations can also be a ploy. If you move to another town with them early in the relationship they have you trapped because you are relying on them for everything and none of your friends or family are around.

If early on you get the impression that there might be opposition to your relationship or an expiry date you are being pressured to make a commitment prematurely.

8. Keep seeing your friends, doing your hobbies and pursuing your interests.

If your new dating partner insists on seeing you every minute, it is a sign of pathology not adoration. The beginning of a relationship is too early to be spending most of your time with someone.

It is one thing to say, "I'm going to the movies with friends." But if someone you have just started dating digs for more detail: which friends, which theatre, which movie, are you going out afterwards? It is best to not give it. "Hiding" information from a narcissist will drive them crazy and they will not want to date you.

On the other hand, if you have few friends, few hobbies and you are bored out of your mind, it may be difficult -- but important -- to not spend every minute with this person. Force yourself to book some time away from them, especially at the beginning.

Why this is important

The ultimate goal of a narcissist is to have you all to themselves. This is part of the control that they have over their partners because the narcissist manages to eliminate everyone else from your life as much as possible. Having only one person in your life makes you very dependent on this person.

Also, you need time at the beginning of a relationship especially to view it from the outside and think about it.

Realize you may want to be "good"
and not realize that you are wired to "obey"
when someone asks you to do something.

In a healthy relationship
your partner will want you to be happy
and having friends, hobbies and interests
is a large part of that.

9. Maintain your private space.

Agreeing to have someone move in right away, or suddenly noticing that one "sleep over" has resulted in the person never leaving is a major red flag. You should make other plans and tell them that you want to go out with your friends and that they can't stay at your place.

Why this is important

This is just one element of how a narcissist moves in and takes control of your life. Suddenly, you will realize that they are living at your place full time. The longer they are there before you stand your ground the more difficult it becomes to maintain your space. Having someone move in right away does not allow time for you to balance this new relationship with the other priorities in your life.

Realize you are fighting biology here.
We instinctively want others around. It feels good to have
company.

Quality relationships are not based on spending as much
time together as quickly as possible. They are based on
mutual respect for each other's lives and priorities.

10. Focus on reciprocity.

If they compliment you, compliment them back. If they ask about you, ask about them. If they do something for you, do it for them.

Why this is important.

Ideally, we all want good relationships. Keeping things in balance is a good starting point for a relationship based on mutual support. By treating them exactly how they treat you, you will become aware of whether or not it "feels normal".

For instance, if they buy you several gifts and it feels abnormal to buy someone you just met that many gifts, you realize that this is a red flag. This method helps you see past the joy you felt in receiving the gifts and puts them in context.

If you feel like you are being disingenuous complimenting them repeatedly, realize that their level of compliments may be abnormal and this is certainly a red flag.

It is easy to get caught up in the whirlwind of a new relationship and suddenly realize that your whole world has changed. With a narcissist it is important to be very aware at the beginning and not let this happen.

Keep in mind
you don't always want relationships
to
"work out"
some of them can be bad for you.

Day-to-Day Narcissism in Action

Narcissists are everywhere. Even if you are lucky enough to not be living with one, involved with one romantically, or reporting to one at work, you still may have one that is difficult to avoid; your neighbour, your sibling, a co-worker, a friend of a friend.

The behaviours of a narcissist are somewhat consistent, but your experience of those behaviours varies greatly depending on your relationship with the narcissist. In the following pages, I'll give some examples of how a narcissist may act in different situations. It is not possible to make a diagnosis, but short of that, it is still valuable to know you *may* be dealing with a narcissist so that you can take steps to protect yourself.

Manipulation

People tend to imbue narcissists will all kinds of special powers and insights into how they are able to fool so many people and why they can get away with such deception. I do not believe this is true. Essentially, they have just ignored the social expectation of honesty and integrity. It is that simple. They have learned to listen and to say what you want to hear unencumbered by honesty or a conscience.

It can be explained by following a simple formula:

How a Narcissist Wins Your Favour

1. **They pay attention to what you are saying.**

   This is incredibly easy to do but something that we often forget to do.

Many of us are already thinking about what we are going to say next instead of listening to what the person is saying. By actually paying attention, the narcissist can ask you more about yourself and show actual interest. This makes you like the narcissist immediately and open up even more because you are being heard.

The next part is when the narcissist begins asking more about the subject matter in a detailed way and becomes more engaged in the conversation. Again, this strengthens the encounter and makes you think that the narcissist is genuinely interested in what you are saying. In addition to that, the narcissist is *collecting useful information about you and what is important to you.*

2. They compliment you.

Narcissists will compliment you on your taste, your appearance or on your astute observation or understanding of something. There will always be a way to compliment you that will make you feel like the narcissist is on your side and that the narcissist is impressed with you. *You will want to be around the narcissist if they make you feel good about yourself.*

3. Connect on a more personal level.

The narcissist will slip something into the conversation that makes them look vulnerable, open, or a victim; or they will share a confidence and suddenly the conversation has deepened into that level of intimacy that feels like you have known this person for a long time. This type of sharing usually results in reciprocation with something personal yourself, because this is social convention and it is expected when someone else shares. *Now the narcissist has real, personal information about you.*

4. Ignore honesty and integrity.

The narcissist is uninhibited by telling the truth. This gives the narcissist a great advantage. When you first meet someone, you are not likely to be wondering, "Is this person telling me the truth?" "Is this person actually interested in what I am saying, or are they trying to manipulate me?" "Does this person actually like the same type of music or are they saying that to build a relationship?" Nor, am I suggesting that you should be, but this is why it is so easy for the average person to be duped. Even professional people familiar with psychology and psychiatry can be duped because we simply do not question EVERY thing that someone says.

Normal people only question something if it sounds outrageous or is different from what we already know. The fact that this individual likes the same things that we like is TOTALLY believable, even if it is a lie. A lie that makes us feel like we have something in common with the narcissist. *Once the narcissist has established this bond with you,* even if someone else says that the narcissist is not nice or not to be trusted, *you are more likely to believe the narcissist than the person who is warning you off.*

Nourishment and Receptacles

All of this friendly behaviour is used to reel you in and convince you that you are the most exceptional and interesting person on the planet. It is necessary for the narcissist to have many admirers around because they are very insecure, despite how aggressively they behave. It is essential that they be constantly nourished by those around them.

> ## *Nourishment*
>
> *Required constantly by a narcissist. This is adoration, hero-worshiping, love, sex and compliments that come from the people in their lives who think that they are wonderful. Narcissists need a* **constant supply of nourishment** *and will have many people in their lives to provide it.*

Ted Bundy, the serial killer, was so personable; he was able to convince many people in the justice system that he was innocent, despite huge amounts of evidence. I'm not suggesting that Ted was simply a narcissist; I'm just trying to say that when you strip away a conscience and there is no moral compass, people can say whatever they want and it is easy to believe what you want to hear. This makes them likeable and very convincing. You immediately become their friend, until you're not.

This false appearance of being the super nice person does not leave any room for the normal behaviours that would naturally occur, causing a build up of anger, hate and rage. In order to receive the adoration that nourishes them, narcissists must never get angry with most of the people they deal with. These superficial relationships are based on lies that allow the other person to like or admire the narcissist. Often the narcissist feels contempt for the person who 'believes' them and therefore must be very stupid (in the eyes of the narcissist).

Since there must be an outlet for all of this pent up negative emotion, the narcissist will direct it at someone who has only mildly provoked them, if necessary. The narcissist may cause conflict in personal relationships and often has one or more *receptacles* for these negative emotions. This receptacle will get picked on and bullied by the narcissist.

The important part here is that they need this receptacle for their anger. It is not that this receptacle has necessarily done anything significant to the narcissist. These perceived slights might be overlooked in normal relationships, but the narcissist desperately needs an outlet so they must find a target. There is a need for this outlet, for this "source" of drama. Some people refer to this as narcissistic supply.

This means that a narcissist is often a very lovable person, until they are not. Once you have given them any reason at all to dislike you, you may become the enemy. If you become the receptacle, the narcissist will focus a huge, ridiculous, amount of energy and time trying to get revenge against you for your perceived slight. This will take the form of trying to embarrass you, hurting you, sabotaging you, anything they can do that will make you look bad and bring you suffering. This vendetta is simply a way to narrowly focus the negative emotions that they must express and in no way proportional to the slight, perceived or otherwise.

Their revenge scheme may include becoming litigious. They love the legal system because it works in their favour. They have no need to be honest and they simply contradict the truth with lies. The court bases many of its conclusions on the premise that the person speaking is not a bold faced liar. In the case of the narcissist, this is not true.

Receptacle

Required by a narcissist. One or more people are required to be the focus of the narcissist's anger. This person or people will be the focus of elaborate and unrelenting revenge scenarios.

It is almost impossible for the other people in your social circle to believe that the narcissist is trying to get "revenge" and there is no sense in even trying to explain it to them. You can't win. This is the narcissist's game and they are willing to commit all of their time and energy to beating you. They are not concerned with lying, hurting anyone or any other moral standard. The other people who think they "know" the narcissist are still getting the charming side of the narcissist and the narcissist is more believable. You, on the other hand, are trying to convince them to dislike someone who makes them feel great about themselves. It just doesn't work.

Great amounts of energy, thought and time are spent on revenge schemes. Narcissists usually have one or more *receptacles* for their hate and anger. When Bob hates, he hates completely. Those that have "wronged" him will be criticized at every opportunity and to every audience. It is important for him to ceaselessly try to discredit this individual, even to people that barely know him.

In most social situations, the person who becomes the receptacle will generally be disliked by the whole group. It may not have started out this way, but it gets worse as time goes on. If this is you, you will find that there are numerous rumours about what you have done and said. There may be stories about what you have done in the past as well. These things may simply be fiction. They may also be exaggerations of small mistakes you have made and the most bizarre is that the narcissist may have done these things and told others that you did them.

32

Without any restrictions on how the narcissist can act, what they can say and what they are willing to do, things can get pretty outrageous: property damage, lying, purposefully doing something that will bring you discomfort; every form of sabotage that the narcissist can dream up.

If you happen to be the receptacle at work, the narcissist will use similar tactics to undermine you. For instance, the narcissist might belittle an idea and then when you do not have the confidence to propose it, they propose it and take credit for it. In general, they try to maintain a superior position over you by undermining you and making you feel self-conscious and off balance. They may spread rumours about you and interfere with your deadlines, accomplishments and ability to do your job. The narcissist might suggest that something that you are wearing is inappropriate right before a big meeting or presentation, undermining your self-confidence.

If you suspect that this dynamic is playing out in your life and you are NOT the target, it is important to keep notes about what is going on so that you can compare what you observe personally to what you have "heard". This is the only way to figure out who the instigator is. Keep in mind that the narcissist can be a skilled liar and many of the things will be said in a way you will believe them. Once a pattern of blaming a certain person for bad behaviour becomes established it becomes more and more believable each time this person does something else outrageous. The person may not have done any of it. This is just a game of revenge for the narcissist.

> *The people who provide nourishment*
> *and those that are the receptacles*
> *see the*
> # *OPPOSITE SIDES*
> *of the narcissist*
> *It is difficult to believe their*
> *descriptions are of the same*
> *individual.*

Many authors have written pieces saying that the receptacle is someone who has seen the truth about the narcissist and so the narcissist must discredit them before they can tell anyone how untruthful and mean the narcissist is. This may be true in some instances and certainly becomes true after the fact.

Bullying at its best, a narcissist can pick on someone until they commit suicide. This has happened many times and the early books on this subject said that most partners of a narcissist either break down completely or simply do not make it out alive. This is changing as more information becomes available and people are more likely to figure out what is going on.

In addition to picking on you, if you are the receptacle, the narcissist will enlist the help of others in your family or social circle. By maintaining the appearance of being this wonderful person, with most of the group, the narcissist is able to turn others against you and the people who have been enlisted will often try to talk to you about your bad behaviour, or decide to exclude you from things. It is not possible to convince others that the narcissist is not their friend. People need to discover this on their own. The best that you can do is to protect yourself.

If you are the target, it is best to try to separate yourself from the narcissist. There is probably nothing that can be done about how the narcissist treats you. Once you have crossed the narcissist, there is no way to get forgiveness from them. They are simply out to destroy you and there is no end point. They need a receptacle for their anger and hate. Letting you out of this role is simply not going to happen. Once the narcissist convinces everyone else to be against you, life can get pretty hard. Know that if you do leave the group, someone else will become the receptacle and the likelihood that the narcissist will be seen for what they are increases.

This dynamic can play out in families wherein one child is the golden child when in fact they are doing everything in their power to destroy a sibling's life. Also, if a parent is a narcissist the family will have a "scapegoat". The scapegoat becomes the receptacle and all of the family members will pick on this person, often without even realizing that this is wrong. When children grow up in an environment wherein one person is picked on, it is difficult for them to realize that this is unacceptable. This is all that they have ever known.

The memory of what childhood was like will differ greatly if one child is the receptacle, or the scapegoat and the other family members are not. Unfortunately, the non-narcissistic parent (if there is one) often becomes one of the perpetrators in this dynamic and does not protect the child. This may be because the other adult knows that they cannot cross the narcissist without negative consequences.

In intimate relationships the partner is usually the receptacle and will move between serving this function, the function of being nourishment for the narcissist and the function of actually taking care of the necessities of life for the narcissist.

You know that you are in a relationship with a narcissist if you are often confused about what the status of your relationship is (switching from your role as receptacle to one that provides nourishment). If you have no idea what is going on and have the suspicion that you may be losing your mind, or at least having difficulty with your memory. If you are starting to feel off-balance you may feel that way because the narcissist wants you to. This is a game for them.

Part of the manipulative nature of a narcissist comes from their ability to make you doubt yourself. When you are living with this type of confusion it can have a major impact on your ability to function normally. This becomes a vicious cycle because as your ability to cope decreases, their attacks have more truth to them and the cycle continues to spiral down.

Arrogance

Narcissists are also known for their arrogance. What must be understood in all of this is that it is a two-way sword. They are boastful and self-conscious all in one unintelligible persona. So much of their interactions with people are as I described above, wherein they try to make themselves appear to be something that they are not, they can't help but be insecure.

A part of your social circle may exhibit arrogance by talking about all of their great accomplishments, downplaying the achievements of others and being a really sore loser. Dave will often agree to something that someone else has suggested and then arrive late, make other plans, decide not to go or forget to make reservations.

> *Known for their arrogance,*
> *what is less understood is*
> *how*
> *insecure narcissists are*

The message is clear: "If I don't win, get my way and everyone agrees to do what I want to do, you will pay with my bad mood and possibly sabotage." If a narcissist wants to control a situation they may blatantly lie saying things like, "I think that concert sold out right away", "The reviews on that movie/restaurant/play were very bad". If you have ever missed a movie, a reservation, or felt really tense all evening without anyone being willing to talk about what is going on, there may be a narcissist in your social circle.

In a work situation, the narcissist will surround themselves with people who agree with them, think that they are wonderful and actively promote them to the other people in the office. These people who provide nourishment are the ones that the narcissist will charm and compliment.

Bob treats the people that report to him at work like simpletons. He sees praise as a way to make them work harder and social humiliation as the result of failure. He must come out on top of everything. Every good idea was his. Every success was a result of his work and every failure is someone else's.

In the family dynamic, nourishment is often the role of the spouse or the favoured child. These people get to dote on the narcissist and support their every utterance. The narcissist cannot go very long without nourishment and can be very demanding. If the people in their lives cannot speak to them right away, they will immediately go in search of someone else to talk to or something else to do.

This entitlement plays out in different ways when the narcissist is a parent. They may feel that they know exactly how a child should look and behave and be very controlling of everything that the child does (dominating narcissistic parent). How the child appears is a reflection of how great the narcissist is as a parent. This can put huge amounts of pressure on the child to achieve amazing things and be the best at what they do. This control over the child is maintained through withholding of affection, if the child does not perform. The parent may also criticize the child and simply be mean if the child does not comply.

The upper limit on these types of accomplishments is that the child cannot outshine the narcissistic parent. Since narcissists must always win, if you are 'better' at something than they are they will be quick to undermine you, tell you, you are a failure, put you down and otherwise shake your confidence. If you shine too brightly you are seen as a direct threat to their superiority.

It is not possible for anyone to stay between the two lines drawn above. You must be "worthy" of affection by making them look good but not too accomplished that you outshine them. The result is a loss of self-confidence, a feeling of abandonment and serious confusion about what the rules are. It is a common experience of children of narcissists to feel like they are "tip toeing" so as not to upset the narcissistic parent.

The other extreme is when the narcissistic parent completely ignores the child as an inconvenience (neglectful narcissistic parent). These children are not cared for, may be expected to take care of the narcissist and often suffer from severe neglect. The parent will let child know that they are unwanted and that they are a complete inconvenience.

The narcissist may use addiction or illness to make sure that all of the attention is focused on them and they are the most important person in the household at all times. This may force some children to take on the role of caregiver, meeting the needs of the narcissist instead of the other way around, as it should be in normal relationships.

The narcissistic need to always be right will be enforced regardless of how this impacts the children or if the rules must keep changing to ensure this. If the parent wants something done a particular way they will get it regardless of how inappropriate it is. This may not make sense to a child that can begin to see that this parent is contradictory and that there is no way to be "right." It is common for the "rules" to change and this keeps the child "in the wrong" a lot of the time and therefore, unsure of themselves.

Emotions

It is common for people to describe narcissists as very sensitive individuals. Knowing whether this is part of their act or whether or not they actually feel sorry for themselves does little to further our understanding of them. If the person you suspect is a narcissist is often crying or sad about how terrible some part of their life has been or is currently, stop and ask yourself if you have ever seen this outpouring of sympathy for someone else.

> ***Don't confuse a play for sympathy as genuine sensitivity.***
>
> ***Narcissists love to play the victim role.***

Great, overwhelming sadness about their own hardship is not the same thing as being "sensitive". This display of vulnerability is one of the ways that they elicit nourishment from others. People feel sorry for them and try to help them and support them and defend their actions because, well, they've had such a hard time.

In social circles, narcissists can be nourished by having the group grant them great leeway in behaviour because of the hard times that they have endured and they will often enlist the support of someone who defends them based on this type of argument.

So, when I say that narcissists don't do emotions, I mean that they don't tolerate them in other people, or more accurately, they decide which emotions are acceptable and which are not.

They have an abundance of hate and rage. They can laugh outrageously at even the mildest of jokes -- when they are trying to ingratiate themselves to the person telling the joke. They feel sorry for themselves a lot. What they don't do is feel empathy. If you are not feeling well, they are quite likely to tell you to, "Suck it up" in blatant contrast to how they expect to be treated when they were playing the sad victim.

Narcissists are very uncomfortable with anyone in the group bringing their problems with them to share with the group. They will make comments about how "needy" someone is even though they may actually be having a tough time. They will not allow anyone to take the limelight away from them. The narcissist may enforce a strict code of only expressing some emotions and enforce it with disapproval.

Narcissists may bring family matters into the workplace to elicit sympathy. They use this as an excuse for not pulling their weight. Also, they may pretend that the boss is picking on them or that they have no choice in how they behave because they have no power. In general, it is not acceptable to bring emotional problems to work. In the event of a tragedy or death in your work group, the narcissist will have a pat remark like, "it is for the best" to derail any further conversation. They don't actually care about the other people in the group and are not comfortable talking about it.

Parents, that are narcissists can take this victim role to herculean levels demanding attention because of illness that is often used as a way to demand that they be taken care of. They may also use this "hard" life that they have had to justify addictions to legal or illegal drugs, again, focusing the energy in the household onto themselves.

A child may serve the narcissist if they can be portrayed as a failure. This gives the narcissist a constant source of pity. "Poor me", my child is such a failure. "My child ruined my life". "My life would be so much better if I didn't have any children." The child then sees itself in a very bad light and this can be traumatizing.

Being "sensitive" as I described above is not the same thing as experiencing or sharing emotions. There is no such thing as unconditional love given by a narcissist. Any emotion is only expressed as an exchange. "I'll show you love if you make me look good," may not be stated, but it is understood or experienced at any rate if you are a child of a narcissist.

Because of this inability to understand that other people have emotions, they don't form normal attachments and the emotional and physical needs of a child may not be met. Any complaints will be seen as a sign of weakness and the child will be criticized for them. Eventually, it will be up to the child to take care of the parent's needs.

Narcissistic parents either are unable to recognize when a child needs affection, comforting or support; or they are unwilling to comfort, but they will not be able to handle this. A favourite line of my mother's when I was growing up was, "If you don't stop crying, I'll give you something to cry about." The meaning was clear. Crying is unacceptable. If you continue to cry I will hit you. If the child expresses anger they will be reprimanded for inappropriate behaviour. It may be seen as disrespectful and it will not be tolerated. Happiness is criticized if excessive. Guilt is often used to control the behaviours.

Another social convention that is bucked by the narcissist is respecting another person's boundaries. This is just seen as an inconvenience to the narcissist, because they feel entitled to go anywhere and do anything. They see you as just one of their servants, not an important person, so there is no reason to respect your privacy or your space.

A neighbour, for instance, might not think twice about entering your yard or your home, borrowing your tools or leaving things on your property. A family member might go into your bedroom or office, go through your things and think nothing of it.

As a superior at work they do not respect "time off", boundaries or privacy and feel like they can read your emails, call you in the middle of the night; come over to your home unannounced. Simply put, they feel justified in invading your privacy. This plays out by having your things examined while you are not home. Being teased publically about private possessions, or creations or experiences.

Relationships

There are many faces to each narcissist. Being dishonest by nature, they become totally different people in different situations. A single individual can be a lover, parent, child, boss, co-worker, friend and a neighbour and how they behave in each situation is somewhat unique. The closer you are to them, the more abuse you will receive because it is more difficult for you to leave. More alarming is that they can switch from "One Side" to the "Other Side" just by deciding to do so. So, even within one relationship you can see two extremes as outlined below.

In the chart below I try to give a visual representation of all of the different types of relationships that you can have with a narcissist. Down the left hand column I describe, in broad terms, a category of relationship and then I show the two extremes that you might experience if you had that connection.

Narcissist is:	One Side	Other Side
Friend/Neighbour/ Co-worker	Admired by Everyone	You are Receptacle
Boss	Assigns Top Projects	Belittles You in Front of Co-workers
Child	High Achiever at all costs	Use Emotional Attachment to Manipulate Parent
Parent	Smothering/Adoring	Neglectful/Resentful
Lover	Soul Mate	Abused Physically and Mentally

Family Gatherings

In social situations, with extended family, narcissists will do their best to control every aspect of any get-together. The time, the theme, the food and entertainment all must be their idea. When others make suggestions for activities, those activities are not included in the event. Even if someone requests that an activity not occur, there is no consideration given to what anyone else wants.

These narcissists have usually learned that they can get their way because when they don't the entire time becomes so uncomfortable that their family has learned to just agree. There are often attempts to create drama like suggesting that someone be left out of a family gathering, or suggesting an activity that one or more family members find offensive. If you don't understand why someone gets to call all of the shots at a family gathering, despite objections, you may be dealing with a narcissist and the others have learned to take the path of the least resistance.

The need for a narcissist to be at the centre of the event plays out in several ways. They will keep bringing the conversation back to themselves; they may become dramatic by leaving the room, feigning a headache or some other ailment, or they will bring up unresolved issues that make people uncomfortable. Narcissists always determine which emotions are acceptable to express and which are not. This is enforced by public humiliation and directly influences how people are willing to behave.

The narcissist loves to come across as the victim and they may use this stance to get their way or to avoid having to contribute to the work involved.

Children

According to the Diagnostic and Statistical Manual of Mental Disorders[1] narcissism is a condition beginning in early adulthood. All teenagers usually go through a particularly narcissistic period where they express many of the traits of being a narcissist. This is a normal part of individuation and is a requirement of separating from the parent and defining oneself as an individual.

So, when I speak of a child that is a narcissist, I'm speaking of an adult child, but the word child is still the most appropriate because it defines your relationship to this individual who is an adult, but is still your child.

This relationship with a narcissist is defined by the child demanding to be seen as the most valuable, the most accomplished and the most loved, despite the fact that there may be other children in the family. The narcissist asserts their superiority by demanding that they get their way. These are the children who refuse to visit unless the parent gives them things, treats them preferentially and allows them to dominate social events. Often, these children are addicted to various legal and/or illegal drugs and will expect the parent to bail them out legally and financially.

They see the parent as one of their resources and want the parent to nourish them, like every other narcissist wants to be served. The child will only want you around if you are serving them in one way or another.

Like I have described about any narcissist, they do not take responsibility for things or love you the way that you love them. Which means that they will criticize your parenting, try to make you feel guilty and blame you for everything that is wrong in their lives. They may use you as a receptacle if you are not willing to meet their demands of being treated preferentially. They will use your emotional attachment against you and treat you as disposable and refuse to see you unless you comply.

Parents

Since narcissists see all of the people in their lives as serving them, it is very difficult to be "beneficial" to them if you are a child. Being the young child of a narcissist can be terribly disorienting. Narcissists can be very damaging to an adult and can be even more destructive to an individual who has no way of knowing that this is not a normal parent/child relationship.

There are many possible combinations of relationships in the parent-child relationship. The same behaviours exist but are expressed differently depending on how the child responds and the parent sees the child. There are two large extremes. First, you may not feel that you were seen or you could not understand why your parents were not that interested in what you were doing. Or, the other extreme is that your parent was overly involved in every detail of your behaviour and appearance. Either extreme might mean that you may have been raised by a narcissist. This results in the children being confused by what the rules are, because they are often changing. It can also result in extreme feelings of loneliness and isolation.

> *If you have a*
> *close personal relationship*
> *with a narcissist,*
> *you are more likely to see both sides*
> *of their personality, this however,*
> *makes it more confusing*
> *because it is hard to understand how*
> *someone can be so lovable and so*
> *mean all in one.*

In general, if you were a child of a narcissist you may have been subjected to extreme verbal threats and raging, including threats of abandonment, public ridicule, inconsistent demands and unpredictable and extreme responses to normal childhood behaviour. This is alternated with periods of warmth and relatively normal behaviour.

Since the narcissistic parent must be the centre of attention at all times they come up with ways to make themselves the most important individuals at all times. This can include anything that focuses the attention on them. They may be outrageous, loud, "dressed to the nines" all of the time. They may wallow in self-pity by being sick, using drugs or alcohol to the point that they need to be taken care of. They may try to be the best at everything or demand this from their child or they may take the victim role.

The narcissistic parent always knows what is right and will not tolerate being questioned. Despite inappropriate and harmful behaviour by the narcissistic parent, often the other parent is not willing to stand up for and defend the child. The other parent, if they are still present, has learned to bend to the will of the narcissistic parent to keep "peace" in the house and this can be very confusing for the child.

In some family situations, one individual will become the "scapegoat" and will be preferentially blamed for everything and picked on by the entire family. This is the receptacle for the entire family, which may have more than one narcissist present. This child will be subjected to being terrorized, excessive teasing, being threatened, insulted and berated in front of others. It is normal for yelling and cursing to the point of scaring the child to be tolerated.

Pure competition, to the point of conflict, is supported by the attitudes and behaviours of a narcissistic parent. All siblings fight to some extent. But since the narcissist is more likely to compare the children to one another, play off their abilities and their efforts against one another and instigate these types of conflicts, the home of the narcissist is much worse.

This can result in a huge imbalance where one child can do nothing right and the other children can do nothing wrong. This conflict is not restricted to siblings. The narcissist may see the child as a competitor for the affections of the other parent and may try to sabotage this relationship so that they "win" with their spouse.

The other extreme is the neglected child who is often ignored and may not even have the basic necessities of life provided. This can result in the child feeling not quite good enough and that they should always try harder. The neglectful parent can be the master of being the victim. They are simply too sick/sad/intoxicated/distraught to actually parent.

Having a narcissist as a parent can leave you emotionally devastated. It is normal to feel like you have to get revenge on your parents (I'm not recommending this). Children of narcissists may see themselves as victims or they may become perpetrators themselves because they believe that the way they were treated was the "right" way to raise a child.

If you recognize the conditions above as similar to those that you were raised in, you need to take a look at your own feelings. It is time to decide if you want to live a life that is free of the pain or if you want to stay in hate, anger and vengeance. If you are ready to move on, I recommend reading as much as you can about narcissism and finding a therapist who specializes in narcissistic behaviours.

Lovers

It can be very difficult to accept that someone you love may be a narcissist. You can think back to all of the nice things that this person has done. You have memories of thoughtful acts, nice gifts, small kind gestures, and yet, you are now alone again and cannot seem to find the person who was so solicitous.

Understand that part of the pathology of narcissism is that they do not love the way that others do. They do not have the emotional attachment to you that you do for them. They may: want you around, like what you can do for them, enjoy having sex with you; but they do not have the same bonds as you do. This gives them all of the power. You need them more than they need you.

Think back to the beginning. A "stereotypical" beginning of a relationship with a narcissist is that is was, "love at first sight." You felt like you had known them forever. They probably shared personal stories of past relationships during which they were hurt. This elicits sympathy and your desire to take care of them. The pace of the relationship was very fast and usually resulted in the loss of independence very quickly.

The narcissist often uses an excuse like; "There is no sense in paying two rents while we are together every night anyway right?" "This place doesn't feel like my home, it feels like yours lets sell and buy one together." "Commuting is wasting so much of your time, quit your job and move in with me and I'll pay the bills until you get another job." "I just got a job offer in a new city, come with me." This happens during the stage when all you have seen is the charming side of them. They have gone above and beyond to be nice, to impress your friends, to be solicitous and thoughtful. But, that ended once it became very difficult to leave.

In romantic relationships the narcissist always gets their way. If there is ever a situation wherein you and your partner both want different things and there is no way to compromise the narcissist always wins. Consider this for a moment, because they are master manipulators and may have convinced you to agree with them.

Have you ever gotten your way? Have you ever had them agree with doing something when it meant that they had to NOT do something that they wanted to do, when they actually had to make a choice? A good example of this is that you want to spend your holidays together, but you want to do different things. There is no way to do both (not enough time possibly, or not enough money). The narcissist always gets their way.

They have a need to assert their superiority and this plays out in arguments that are more about "winning" than they are about discussing issues (see part on arguing with a narcissist). In competitive pursuits, the narcissist will become angry or despondent if you are beating them. If necessary they will become violent to "win". Also, if there is a possibility that you will outshine them in some arena, they will sabotage your efforts interfering with your confidence and possibly directly doing things to make sure that you are not successful.

Another characteristic is how narcissists behave in periods of crisis when you actually need them. For instance, if you come home from work with bad news, how do they react? They despise having to "give" in a relationship and needing to support you is off-putting. Often they will be too busy with something important that they must do, will find an excuse to leave or simply attack you for not handling it better and for being so needy.

In addition to that, many narcissists use sex as a weapon, masturbate a lot and are unfaithful. If your sex life is unsatisfying and you often feel like your needs are not being met, this might be one of the battlegrounds in your relationship.

Also, nothing is ever their fault. If they forget, you should've reminded them. If there are problems at work it is because of the jerks that they have to work with. If something is done wrong, the information was insufficient. It is never their fault.

Unlike healthier relationships that are all give and take, that leave you feeling supported and loved, a narcissist does many of the same behaviours and then simply leaves. This may be emotional abandonment or physical abandonment but you are not supported and loved. This can destroy your self-esteem, which makes it more difficult to leave, but more on that later.

As you look at this summary, it becomes obvious that almost everyone that you know has at least one or two of these traits. The distinction comes in when it is an overall pattern of not caring about other people. So, make sure you consider the entire individual. Before you start to treat them like they are a narcissist, make sure that they have

shown lack of empathy

the hallmark of the characteristics that distinguishes them from someone who is just really, really arrogant and self-centered.

Part 2: What Do I Do Now?

So, now we know what to look for. If we determine that someone significant in our lives may be a narcissist, we will need to learn how to deal with them. I understand that many of you will immediately think that I am going to persuade you to leave. My experience is that many, many, people who are with narcissists love them dearly and just hope that their better attributes will someday be all that they see. This information can be helpful either way.

There is a certain amount of relief that will descend on you when you realize that the person that you are dealing with may be a narcissist. Most of us do not come to the conclusion that the other person may be sick -- at least initially. We look closely at ourselves and try to determine what we did wrong, how we could have reacted differently and how we can make things different next time.

Knowing that most, if not all of it, was not your fault can make a huge difference. Also, it is a pathology, so there are things that you can do to make the relationship more manageable. I begin with the most important part, how to protect yourself as much as possible and prepare to leave if this is what you want. Then, I try to elucidate a typical type of argument, one that you may have already had in the past. I speak to finding a modicum of sanity if you decide to stay, talk about the reality that you may be reading this on behalf of someone else that is tangled up in a narcissistic relationship and finally notes on how to begin recovery and deal with these people long term.

Depending on the type of relationship that you have with the narcissist, how you handle the situation will differ greatly. There is one thing that seems immutable, the behaviour of the narcissist is not going to change. Repeat after me...

"The best predictor of future behaviour is past behaviour."

The reason that this comes up so often is that the narcissist can be very charming and exciting: the drama, the fights, the certainty of the narcissist, can all be very passionate. Other relationships may appear boring and not as interesting as being with a narcissist.

By the end of this chapter you should be able to see your relationship better. You should learn how to observe how you are being manipulated, understand why discussions do not lead to resolution of the issues and finally how to set boundaries that are clear and will stop the narcissist from using you as a receptacle or for nourishment.

Protecting Yourself From the Narcissist

If you have recognized someone from your life as likely a narcissist there are some things that you can do to protect yourself from their particular type of influence. Protecting yourself is a step-by-step process. Begin by determining whether or not you are happy right now with your life as it is. This seems like a broad way to look at things, but narcissists affect your entire life. This is way larger than your relationship with the narcissist. Except, of course, if you only encounter the narcissist rarely.

If you are often confused, lonely, angry or questioning your sanity; how many friends do you think you'll have? What is the quality of the relationships that you will have? How well are you sleeping? Are you taking care of yourself? How are you performing at work? Are you engaging in your hobbies, passions or interests? Are you content with your life? If your are enjoying your life as it is, you are done. If not, go to the next step.

1. The first thing that you need to do is accept that things will not change.

This might sound easy, but it is not. One of the reasons that you have been in this relationship for so long is that you have come to believe that this narcissist will be the wonderful person you see for brief periods. They will love you back. The arguments and drama will become less frequent and you will be living the life that you have put your heart and soul into creating.

Exercise 1   Acceptance

Repeat after me,

"The best predictor of future behaviour is past behaviour."

Just for practise, say it again, "The best predictor of future behaviour is past behaviour." Make it your mantra.

I know that it is difficult to give up on hope, but the truth is they are who they are. The behaviour that makes you crazy will still be occurring in the future whether you are there or not. Accept that things are not going to get better, promises won't be kept this time or next time either, the pain, the ups and downs will continue.

Keep in mind that if you are deciding to leave, the narcissist will promise anything. When you are ready to walk out the door, the narcissist will turn on the charm. Unencumbered by truth, caring about whether or not they hurt you and armed with the knowledge of what you like, they pour it on. This is the construct that you love. This is the person you were hoping to stay with. This person does not exist. They are an illusion, created by an actor wishing to deceive you. It makes it very hard to leave.

They will agree to counseling, taking the holiday that YOU want, changing their behaviours, ANYTHING, until you decide to stay or until they get bored and then they will revert to who they are -- again. "The best predictor of future behaviour is past behaviour." When you can honestly say to yourself that you know that your relationship will not improve, it is time to move to the next, not so easy step, acceptance.

2. The second thing that you need to do is to accept what is.

Your goal is to accept the facts as they stand. This does not make everything OK. This does not mean that the pain that you have been through is not real. This does not mean that you should forget what happened. Simply put, it did happen. There is no way to go back and change it. You cannot rewrite how you acted or what the outcome was. They still did what they did.

Accepting your behaviour as a fact cannot be brushed aside. You were a trusting person and a loving person (even if you did some things that you wished you hadn't). But, the reality of it all is that you are in this mess because you loved and trusted someone. That does not make you a bad person. That does not make you a stupid person. That does not make you a weak person. It just makes you a caring, loving person who happened to trust someone who turned out to be a narcissist. It happened. Accept that it happened.

Acceptance is not easy. When you find yourself rewriting history by saying things like, "If I had remembered to shut the door, the dog wouldn't have run out" or perhaps something more directly related to the narcissist, you know that you have not accepted what happened. Your mind is still more comfortable with "what should've been" rather than what was. When you remember the dog incident, forgive yourself. Recognize that you are human, that you made a mistake and tell yourself you still love yourself. Let it slip away. You left the door open -- full stop.

Exercise 2   Letting Go

An exercise that can help move this along is to hold an object that can be dropped. The physical sensation of letting something fall from your hand is not only symbolic, but it can help to remind you to let the past be the past. Let it go. So, in the future when you hear yourself saying, "I should've...." pick the object up and state what actually happened and before you mind goes to where you "should've done something different" let the object drop.

It can be particularly effective to drop something that makes a distinct noise like a bag of beans that makes a crushing sound when it hits, or an empty can that clangs on a hard surface. The reason that this is desirable is that when these thoughts occur and you are not near your object, you can visualize dropping it anyhow and remember the noise that it makes when it hits. This sends your brain off on a new pathway and stops you from repeating the regret or the story about what you "wish" happened.

You know that you have been successful with accepting what happened when you stop fantasizing about how things could've been. When you realize that you no longer make excuses for what happened or try to rewrite history in the way that you remember it.

The anxiety about what has happened will start to slip away and a calm acceptance of what happened replaces the wish for something different.

You are here now, despite what happened. It is only possible to be here today if you are not stuck in thoughts about yesterday. You are only able to make changes now, today, right at this moment, so lets not waste it thinking about all of the bad that happened and wishing that it weren't true.

53

Exercise 3 Observing Yourself

Think of a small irritation or oversight that your narcissist does and try to accept that this is who this person is and that they'll keep doing it. Let's start real small like leaving the milk on the counter, while away at work. If this particular example is not a problem in your home, pick something else. It is preferable if the narcissist is not physically present for this exercise i.e. we're not thinking about having a fight or something that they say or physically do to you. But we want it to be something that you have discussed, something small that you do not like and go through this exercise with that example in mind.

For example, you walk in and the milk is out. Physically stop moving and be still. Notice your emotional reaction. Notice how that reaction is perceived in your body. Try to describe the sensations in your body without using any descriptors for emotions. For instance, do not describe it as, "I am miffed". Try to describe how your body feels when miffed instead. Like, I can feel a hot energy rising in my chest or I've noticed my shoulders are up around my ears or my hands are clenched. Experience this sensation, even if it is quite mild. Do not tell yourself that it is OK or not OK. Do not try to explain it at all, just experience the sensation and pay attention to what it is.

This is a good thing to write down after the exercise because it helps you tune into all of the messages that your body is giving you.

After you have fully paid attention to your reaction, tell yourself that the only meaning that you can take from the milk being on the counter is that it was left out. This has no larger meaning. It is easy to get sidetracked here and to make it about the relationship, your importance in their life, how inconsiderate they are and all of those things, but it is not. It is just a fact that the milk gets left out. Period. This is not a battle, this is the truth.

If you can get to this place, the first thing that you'll notice is that other "possibilities" for resolution come to the surface. Since it no longer becomes making them change or act differently-- you can't-- it comes to what are the other solutions? For instance, a smaller milk container so that not so much milk goes to waste, or sterilized milk that can be left at room temperature -- you get the idea. We are trying to move away from blame and then the next step, which is trying to make them change, because they will not.

Try this for as many of the small irritations as possible. The main things to focus on are:

1. pay attention to how your body reacts to the situation
2. state the facts at hand (this happened, this is happening)
3. do not go into any explanations or stories about why this happened/is happening (like it is because they don't respect me, or because they hate me or are ignoring me etc.)
4. focusing on only the facts, see if there are new ways to find a solution or accept that there is nothing that you can do but accept it (buy milk more often, from our example)
5. let it go as just "the way it is", because that is the truth.

When you are able to perceive these small irritations without getting into a full-blown crisis about your relationship, congratulate yourself. Some of their control over you is falling away, move to something harder.

There are several benefits to this exercise. First, it gets you in touch with how much emotional energy is being expended in a day. By stopping and paying attention to how your body reacts, you begin to understand the stress, the tiredness and the body aches that you have.

Another benefit is that it starts to change the way you think. In normal relationships, if you say to someone, "It really bothers me that you do that", they do their best to not do it. This is not true of a narcissist. The narcissist is more likely to do these things, especially when they need an emotional hit, which they get by fighting. By only considering changes that you can make, rather than hoping that they will change, you give yourself the power to not be drawn into the drama. You begin to step out of the role of the receptacle. The milk was left out, I'll need to buy more -- no drama.

Finally, it shifts your focus from, "They should remember to put the milk away" to "The milk will often be left out". This is an acceptance of how things are, rather than a hope for change. Instead of swimming in a sea of confusion and being overtaken by waves of emotion, you can come up for air, reconnect with your sanity and see the shore.

When you are comfortable with the small, thoughtless or selfish things that they do, move onto actual encounters with them. This is way more difficult and it is OK to never master it. All we are trying to achieve is acceptance that this is the way that they are and hopefully break your own pattern of how you react.

3. The third step to take is to become the observer of the relationship.

All relationships narcissists have serve them. They behave in certain ways to get what they want. Once you know this, you can ask yourself,

"What do they want right now?"

This is a powerful question because it helps you see them for the manipulators that they are.

When they are acting moody and unpleasant because the activity that they wanted to do was not agreed to by everyone, ask yourself, "What do they want right now?" Suddenly, it becomes apparent that they are trying to manipulate everyone into doing what they want. They are training their friends to do what they want or suffer the consequences.

If you find yourself at work, feeling self-conscious, because a narcissist has just told you that your idea was not worth pursuing, ask yourself, "What do they want right now?" This is a powerful tool, because it allows you to observe what happens next. If they tell you it is a bad idea and then propose it at the meeting (because you thought it wasn't good enough to propose) you will never let that happen again.

If they are causing discord in your life, it makes it easier to see that they like the drama. They will have at least one receptacle at work or in a social situation. Pay attention to who gets blamed for everything and see if there is any actual evidence or just a lot of rumours.

Much the same way that you learned to observe the milk on the counter, you are now trying to step back and observe how the relationship, actual encounters, with your narcissist work.

Exercise 4   Observing Them

Observe and ask yourself, "What do they want right now?"

Every narcissist has several tactics that they use to get what they want. So let's look at what they might want, and some of the ways that they get it. There are three major categories of needs: having a physical need met such as food, a clean house, laundry; having an emotional need met; and having their egos stroked. Not every person in their lives fills all of these needs, but if you are in their life you are filling at least one of these. Read the sections below and try to determine which category or categories of needs you fill.

a. Necessities of Life

In a nutshell, they want someone else to do their work for them. If you do more "favours" for this person than they reciprocate, then this is at least part of your role.

A neighbour or friend or co-worker may be asked to do favours by the narcissist. Helping move furniture, fix something, borrowing equipment, editing an email, on and on. The hallmark of the narcissist is they are rarely, if ever, are available to reciprocate.

If you are the one that takes care of things like meals and laundry, they often get this by making you feel like you are lazy or selfish if you do not do it for them. They will have a reason that they can't do it like, they earn the most money so this is your part, they have a bad back, they are so stressed from work or they are not feeling well. Or, they are not able to do it properly. There may be a basket of these, but the idea is that they are trying to make you feel like you should be contributing more or that they aren't capable.

To help you observe, you need to ask yourself,

"What do they want right now?"

So if they say something like, "You never make my favourite meal anymore" recognize that they want you to cook. By labeling it as "my favourite meal" they are creating a situation wherein only YOU can make it. They are also criticizing you for not making it more. All that they really want in this example is to be fed and for you to do the cooking.

My personal favourite is when they exaggerate and try to make it appear that they are actually doing more than you are, you just don't appreciate all that they do. When in fact they don't. It is just another set of lies.

A similar tactic is to do a very basic task wrong. For instance, they might pile the dishes into the dishwasher in a way that the water spray won't get them clean, or put the pots and pans away slightly dirty or the laundry slightly wet. When you visit the question, "What do they want right now?" it is clear that they don't want to have to do the work. If they are 'untrainable' and will not do it properly, or worse, do it in a way that damages things, then you have to do it.

Forgetting is often used. Despite reminders, notes, electronic alarms and the like, they will "forget" things that they don't want to do. Simply observed, "What do they want right now?" is of course, to not have to do what ever it is that they've been asked to do.

Keep in mind that they are not likely incapable. They manipulate people so that they don't have to do things. There is a difference. Observe how much work you do on their behalf. Are you the one that meets this need? Are you the one that has been convinced that you need to do it all? **Do they do anything on your behalf?** (Be careful of the money issue here. They are not earning money "for you" if you are not in charge of how it is spent.) No judgment here, just observation.

b. Receptacle

Another thing that the narcissist needs is an emotional fix. Observation alone confirms that narcissists need to be in conflict a lot of the time, relative to other people. It could be because they do not feel the love and connection with people that others feel and they need the anger and rage to feel anything. It could be that they enjoy the conflict directly. I can't say, but what I know for sure is that they create drama intentionally and need a receptacle for their negative emotions. Anger and hate must come out.

The receptacle is the target of their anger, the

focus of their revenge vendettas and is in their life as a pressure valve. If they are mad at you or blame you a lot this is at least part of your role.

This can happen even if you barely see the narcissist. They need a target so they will use you if they have even the slightest reason.

'Pushing your buttons,' has become a well-know phrase for doing things that intentionally make someone angry. Be it the milk we discussed above or 'forgetting' things or many of the other insults and put downs that they use, a narcissist knows how to pick a fight.

Try to observe this process. It will be very difficult at first, but go back to the exercise above where you become still and try to notice the sensations in your body. Observe what it was that caused the body sensations. This is a process that will develop over time, so don't be too hard on yourself. Try to see the beginning of these situations by being still. Don't speak. Don't react. Focus on paying attention to your body.

The ultimate goal is to just not let them upset you, but this may not be achievable and I must caution everyone at this point. If there is a possibility that your narcissist will become violent be very careful with this approach. If they can't get their emotional fix by insulting you, accusing you, attacking who you and having you engage them in an argument, they may get desperate enough to physically hurt you. Don't risk this.

When you notice that your body has reacted in a way that signifies there is conflict, ask yourself, "What do they want right now?" You may find that all they want is the fight. There might be another need that is going unmet like sex, food or chores, but sometimes they just want the fight.

c. Nourishment

Narcissists tend to be so insecure that they need to be admired almost constantly. If you tell them how great they are, especially when it is not reciprocal, this is at least part of your role.

Some people serve all three roles at various times and I don't need to say that this situation is very emotionally abusive. So, if you recognize that you do all three, please do what you can to take care of yourself.

There is no question that narcissists need to be told how special they are. It is not enough to say, "good job". It must be the best job ever. They are the most beautiful, talented, skillful, engaging....(I think I'm going to be sick if I keep this up) If this is your role in their lives, you will notice that they are telling you about something that they did, some new way that they dress or do their hair, something they said, accomplished or got noticed for, on a rather frequent basis.

If you pay even more attention to the narcissist, you will notice that they don't congratulate or acknowledge what you have accomplished, or at least not very enthusiastically. This is an important realization, because we all want to celebrate accomplishments with our loved ones. This is a need that you have that they might not meet.

When they are telling you about something that you should be proud of or impressed by, ask yourself, "What do they want right now?" Recognize that this is one of your roles in your relationship. You are there to provide adoration and nourishment for their fragile ego.

There may not be any tactics that they use to get you to stroke their egos. Chances are that if you play this role in their lives, you do it willingly. But, they still need you to provide this unconditional adoration, so as long as you are providing it, you are their source.

Once you have determined your role, you can decide if you want to continue or not. If you are the receptacle, and only know the narcissist casually, you may decide to avoid all contact. If you do things for the narcissist, you may want to stop. You will be amazed how quickly they no longer want to see you. If you provide nourishment, you can decide if you want to continue this one sided relationship.

4. The fourth step is to stop meeting their needs.

If there is a specific thing that they want from you, try not to provide it. For instance, you might say, "I don't feel like fighting". If you can keep repeating this, after a barrage of verbal abuse, you can observe how much they need the fight. If they want you to do something, you might say, "I have to go do an errand, or I'm tired". If they want nourishment, say as little as possible. See what happens. You are purposefully making yourself less valuable to them. You are not meeting their needs.

This is when they'll pull out the big guns to try to get what they want. Often, if they can't get their other needs met, they will resort to starting a fight. The emotional hit can hold them over for a while. Once again, I'll caution you if your narcissist might become violent, don't push it.

Also, you must prepare yourself to be replaced. If you no longer "adore" them they will find someone who will. If your ultimate goal is to end the relationship, realize that being replaced is a good thing.

Stop Giving them What they Want

Since narcissists see everyone in their lives as serving them, a sure-fire way of getting them out of your life is to stop giving them what they want. When you become less valuable, they will no longer go to you for their supply of drama, ideas, nourishment, or whatever it is that you provide for them. I go into much more detail later on how to do this.

5. Demand to be Treated Properly

Since narcissists have no respect for boundaries it will be important to set up limits for them to follow. These need to be clearly outlined and probably written down. The value of this is that once you have set up guidelines, you can simply ignore any communication that occurs outside of the predetermined rules. There is no drama or conflict, you have been specific and if the guidelines aren't followed, you just ignore the person.

State when they can call/text/email/ or arrive at your door. Be clear where they can see you, for instance, it might not be appropriate at work, or at home - maybe just at the mall or a coffee shop. Clearly outline when they can expect a response. Demand that they treat you with respect when communicating with you.

If any of your guidelines are not followed: shut the door, hang up the phone, walk away, avoid contact or whatever is the most appropriate way to avoid drama and give as little response as possible. Focus exclusively on whether or not they have been following the rules instead of responding emotionally -- an emotional response is what they are seeking.

"You can only see and hear them under the guideline rules."

Ignore them otherwise.

6. Make plans on where to go.

Ultimately, you want to move out. [if you do not want to move out, read this, just for kicks] So, you must make arrangements. This can be very practical like opening your own bank account, getting a credit card in your name, speaking to friends or family about your plan to move out. You may be able to rent a place to stay or find a shelter that can keep you for a longer term.

Do not move out yet.
(if possible)

The narcissist must always feel like they have won. They must think that they are the one on top. They are the smartest person in the room and everything that occurred was because they planned it that way. They are in control blah, blah, blah. If you leave them they might pursue you for a very long time. This is a dangerous period because the person who shows up is the one that you love. Do not let them know that you are planning on leaving. The idea is to just become less valuable to them so that they want you gone.

So bide your time. Continue to not meet their needs. Don't get pulled into jealousy when they start replacing you. Expect them to have to "work late" and/or out of town. Expect to find evidence of an affair. They want to get caught. They want you to fight for them. That way they keep you on the hook fighting for the relationship, doing as much as possible to keep them happy.

Find support outside of the relationship to help you get through this part of this transition. It will be incredibly painful, but if you have been observing your relationship you should realize what it looks like and what it will always look like.

I understand that it can be almost impossible to tear yourself away from someone you love. I also understand that many narcissists can be very engaging, nice, solicitous people when they want to be. Some of the things that I discuss will help you keep your sanity if you want to stay in the relationship or they will help you to see the relationship more clearly if you decide to leave.

Many of us have suffered through a relationship with family members that are narcissists. Yes, I know that you love them. Yes, I know that you care about them. The question is, can you stay with them and love and care for yourself? This is a personal decision except when other people are involved.

If you have children in your care, it is very difficult to protect them from the influence of a narcissist. Also, you may be excluding other loved ones, people who can truly love you back, by keeping the narcissist in your life. Many people will not chose to stay in your life if it means that they are constantly on a roller-coaster of emotions worrying about your well-being and if you are OK. All things considered, you can use the information to stay or to go, but at the very least, use it to protect yourself as much as you can.

Remind yourself,

**"The best predictor of future behaviour
is past behaviour. "**

Remember what your life has been like.

Observe the situation and ask,
"What do they want right now?"
Don't give it to them.

Know that:
**they are who they are,
life has been unpleasant,
they are acting this way so that you'll
try to get them back**
and that
you don't want them back.

Wait.

They will try to end the relationship.

Agree.

Move out.

Arguing with a Narcissist

Narcissists love conflict and one of the ways they can make you crazy is the tactics that they use when they argue. Your narcissist will be familiar with all of the phrases that you use to start a conversation that will be uncomfortable. Since they enjoy conflict and do not want to take responsibility for anything, they will try to derail the conversation. This has the added benefit of being a game for them and they enjoy avoiding the topic that you want to discuss.

There are several tactics that are very common, so I'll outline those. I'm sure there are other things they can do, but becoming aware of some of the patterns will take you a long way towards understanding what is going on.

1. Attack

Attacking is one of the most common approaches. It does not matter what you want to discuss, they will attack you. If they can undermine your self-confidence, redirect the conversation or get you to back off completely so much the better.

How this is done.

There are several tactics, belittling you for "needing to talk", criticizing you for bringing up something that has been discussed previously (even if it was never resolved). They will also make personal attacks about you, your appearance, your abilities, your friends -- wherever they know that you are vulnerable or self-conscious.

2. Misdirecting the conversation.

Trying to get you off topic, or upset you so much that you can't think straight is the goal, once an argument has begun.

How this is done.

They can say things that they know upset you; make reference to previous arguments during which there was no resolution; change topics by focusing on one small aspect of what you are saying, instead of the point, or simply just treat the conversation as an inconvenience.

3. No Empathy

There is no concern about what you want to talk about. They do not care why you are upset or try to draw you out. They are trying to shut you down. They will use taunts that demonstrate that they think very little of you.

How they do this:

Belittling your concern. Letting you know that what you want to talk about is not important to them.

4. Playing a Game

This is all about winning for them. They are not interested in knowing what you want to talk about or concerned about how you are feeling. This is just sport. They are going to end this conversation without having to address your worries.

How they do this:

A combination of all of the tactics are used to misdirect the conversation, they try to get you to a place where you are feeling so insecure that you do not want to pursue it. They make the conversation about you instead of about them. They will cut you off, change topics and attack as a way of confusing you so that it becomes more difficult to focus on what you want to say.

5. Saying Outrageous Things

This is twisting something that you have said and making it sound ridiculous. You may be concerned that they did not do something that you asked. Instead of directly commenting on your question, they could say something like, "Am I supposed to do everything you want now?" which purposefully overstates the situation to the point of ridiculousness.

How they do this:

They take a small element of what you are talking about and expand it to make it not only ridiculous but also indefensible. It may not have even been the point of what you were saying just part of the thought. Then they use this construct to point out how foolish what you were saying is.

6. Prefabricated Lies

When ultimately cornered, they use a practiced lie. Narcissists lie easily and can do it with very little effort, so it is not always possible to tell that they are lying.

How they do this:

They wait until they can use the exact phrase in a way that it has been practiced. They then state without any hesitation what you want to hear.

Excerpt from *Miss Dial*

Let me use a conversation from a movie to illustrate these points. This is from, "Miss Dial" so spoiler alert!!! What I am about to say gives away a lot of the plot.

This argument begins when the protagonist is confronting her boyfriend about something that one of her friends has told her.

She says, "I think we need to talk."

He replies, "Oh no, here we go."

> *This is an example of an "attack" posture. There is a total lack of concern about the fact that she wants to talk. He shows no genuine consideration for how she is feeling. He lets her know through his tone of voice that this is inconvenient for him. Narcissists do not "do emotions" so he doesn't care about how she feels.*

In the movie, we can see (the protagonist cannot see because she is on the phone) that he is amused. He has been caught. Let the game begin. He is taking delight in his ability to handle this situation.

He is using the stance, "The best defense is a good offense". This undoubtedly started out as a sports metaphor. Picture hockey. The best way to win is to focus on scoring goals, rather than tying to keep the other team out of your end. The narcissist uses this attack stance to gain an emotional advantage in the discussion. He keeps the protagonist off balance by repeatedly attacking her so that it is more difficult for her to confidently stand her ground.

He says, "What's the matter, am I not tuning into your feelings again?"

> *This statement is an example of having no empathy. He is trying to belittle her. This is a taunt*

70

meant to undermine her self-confidence and hurt her. It is also misdirection. If he can get her to answer this question instead of pressing on, she has been derailed.

He has not given her a chance to speak yet. He is trying to undermine her before she begins.

This is part of the game playing strategy. I have not left anything out of the conversation; he has simply not allowed her to talk. He is trying to attack and undermine her confidence so that she cannot say what she wants to say.

She tries to gather some strength and says a few small comments, " I don't know. I don't know how to say this." She is trying to get her thoughts together so that she can start again.

He cuts in, "Let's cut to the chase."

By cutting her off here, he is interfering with her ability to restart and actually say what she wants to say. He is playing a game still, by interrupting her thoughts. He is letting her know that he is impatient. He doesn't want to talk and she hasn't been able to say anything yet, so he is emphasizing this by saying that she should just get to the point.

She says, "Someone saw you with that girl from your work, Amanda something."

As soon as she says why she is concerned, he attacks again, not addressing the content of her question, but the source of it.

"Who saw me?" he asks attacking. "Your friend Samantha, with the fat ass?"

She says, "No, it was someone else, look it doesn't matter who, she saw you having lunch with Amanda"

Several elements are all used at once here. He is attacking. He is misdirecting the conversation by changing the topic. He is trying to put her on the defensive by insulting her friend. This is a ploy, a red herring, and a way of avoiding the conversation. These are often more personal than this and can be effective at changing the conversation completely around and making it about you defending yourself. He does not address her question about being seen having lunch with another woman.

If she had started to defend Samantha, or point out that she doesn't have a fat ass, or that it is rude to be describing someone that way, he would have won early in the conversation.

He says, "So what am I not allowed to have lunch with someone I work with now?"

This is obviously ridiculous and is outrageous on purpose.

She replies, "She said it looked suspicious."

He replies, "How exactly do you eat lunch suspiciously? Was I making a shifty eye motion? Or did a man in a trench coat drop off a brief case at my table?"

This is obviously ridiculous and is outrageous on purpose.

Mixed in with these outrageous statements is actually a true statement, but it is buried in all of the ridiculous ones so it is easy to classify it as something that is ridiculous.

"You got me. I have been boning Amanda and afterwards I thought we would have lunch in a public place."

Then he goes back to ridiculous statements:

"So, that everyone could see me groping her tits."

"Oh, and did your friend Sarah tell you that I left a used condom in the booth? I meant to grab it I just didn't have time."

The protagonist stays focused and asks straight out, "Are you cheating on me?"

He turns it around, "I thought you trusted me?"

> *The insinuation here is that he is not in the wrong. She is in the wrong for not trusting him.*

Then he says, "I can't believe you need me to say it."

> *He takes another jab at her. He is trying to show her she is somehow deficient. It is her "need" to hear it that is the problem. She should not be so "needy".*

> *My favourite bit of this whole scene is that he waits until he can use a pre-rehearsed phrase.* ***There is a whole shift in his facial expression, his tone of voice and his attitude. This is the hallmark of the pre-rehearsed phrase.*** *He has practiced this. It stands out because it is the only time that he is not attacking her. This is an outright lie. He grins when she accepts his line.*

"Baby, I would never cheat on you and you know that."

Immediately, he goes back on the attack, "I should be mad at you right now."

Then, he lays in about her friend again, using the same wording as he did earlier about her other friend.

> *It is important that a narcissist separate you from your friends, because it gives them more power and control. Often, after being with a narcissist for a while, people realize that they hardly ever see the friends that they do still have and that they have fewer friends. This is not an accident.*

By being aware of the way that a narcissist argues it allows you to focus on what you are trying to say and actually stick to the topic at hand. This will not necessarily make it possible for you to discuss things. Any attempt that you make to get them to talk about what you want to talk about will likely be countered.

Often, if the narcissist cannot derail you, lie directly to address your concern or get out of the conversation another way, they will just stop talking to you. This will either be by hanging up or leaving the room. Some narcissists will resort to violence so be careful in any conflict situation.

How Do I Warn Someone that they May be With a Narcissist?

It is very difficult to watch someone you like be involved with one. We all know how they got there. Initially, the narcissist is "the perfect soul mate" and showers them with affection and attention. Then, as the relationship progresses more and more of the pathology starts to show.

There will be mentions of multiple arguments and confusion about events. Increasingly, your friend will want to stay home or will cancel activities at the last moment. Most notably, the relationship will either be "on the rocks" or "wonderful" when you talk to your friend and this will keep changing back and forth. Often, plans will be cancelled because your friend needs to stay home and tend to the relationship.

The narcissist can appear in many different ways to your friend's family and social group. Some narcissists will maintain the charming side when dealing with everyone that knows their partner. Some will immediately offend everyone and some will just be unavailable for most social activities, or any combination of the above.

1. Blurting out, "I think you're with a narcissist" is not going to work. For that matter, it may be
exactly the wrong thing to do. Thing is, the oxytocin that is produced in massive amounts during intimate encounters strengthens bonding. When bonding starts between two individuals one of the effects it has is to enhance the "us" versus "them" feelings and any attacks directed at the narcissist will fortify the narcissist's position. You become the enemy and the narcissist will be skillful at making sure that your relationship with your friend diminishes.

2. Where you can be helpful is by truthfully answering questions -- when asked. It is a societal norm to
lie to one another about what we know about relationships. Think of how many people you know who are having affairs and how no one tells the spouse. I was floored when I divorced my husband and

people I barely knew came out of the woodwork to tell me things they had known for years.

But, I was more hurt by my closer acquaintances that had known things and decided not to discuss them with me. The argument went something like this, "We thought you knew and we were helping you save face." Unfortunately, when you are involved with a narcissist and being lied to by the narcissist and then everyone around you is lying as well, it can be kind of crazy making. I had never actually known what most people thought of him, even though I had confided in some of these people about how awful it was.

Keep your statements to the facts. When I confided that we argued a lot, it would have been nice to have someone say, "you seem to be arguing more than normal". Or, "he seems to be cruel", or, "I don't think I could be in a relationship when someone was that mean to me". It is not helpful to hear, "I'm so sorry to hear that." "You should get counseling." "Everyone argues." These may all be true, but when you know that there is more pathology, it would be helpful to point to facts. A person in a relationship with a narcissist needs clarity above all else. You can see the outside of the relationship and if you can point to something, let them know -- when asked.

3. Never join the narcissist in humiliating your friend or making jokes at their expense. This is a common tactic that makes people feel inferior, unloved and picked on. Nothing is worse than having to help people taunt you. Just because your friend is laughing along does not mean that they are enjoying the insults and putdowns, even if they are in the form of a "joke". This also fortifies the narcissist. When your friend tries to ask for the taunting to stop, the finger will be pointed at you, you laughed as well.

4. Be aware that the narcissist is likely using manipulation to get what they want. This includes withholding affection, money, conversation and anything else they have power over. The person will have become very sensitive to this dynamic either consciously or unconsciously, so any attempt to manipulate them by saying, "If you don't break off the relationship I

will no longer be your friend", normalizes the behaviour. In other words, your friend may think, "Even friends withhold attention if I don't do what they want. This must just be the way that people get what they want." Giving a friend an ultimatum plays into the narcissist's hands.

5. The best thing that you can do for your friend is to stay in touch, give facts and information when they are requested and focus as much as you can on your friendship, rather than on their other relationship.

6. If the relationship gets bad enough, or an opportunity presents itself, it might be time to say that it sounds like their lover might be exhibiting some of the traits of a narcissist and direct them to some resources on the topic.

7. At the end of the day, most people have to go through the painful realization on their own and this is when friendships are the most important because they will need a lot of support to reclaim their sense of self, get their self-confidence back and try to rebuild their lives. Knowing as much as you can about narcissists is very valuable at this point so you can help them understand what happened.

Recovering from a Narcissistic Relationship

As you begin to see the relationship that you have with the narcissist more clearly, healing begins. Just knowing that you are not losing your mind and it is not a "normal" relationship can do wonders towards restoring your self-esteem and helping you begin to see that you were not actually the cause of all of the problems.

It is also important to understand that being in a relationship causes a certain amount of bonding. We have all laughed at videos of little ducklings following inappropriate things around. Ducks and geese both imprint on the first moving object they see upon hatching. Imprinting is designed to ensure survival since the hatchling must rely on its mother for both food and protection. Oxytocin is responsible for this behaviour.

> *Several hormones make it*
> *very difficult*
> *to end an intimate relationship*

Oxytocin is one of a cocktail of chemicals that are produced in humans in response to social activities, touch, and in larger amounts during intimate encounters. Oxytocin ensures that we bond with others, especially intimate partners. It also makes us feel safe and it is responsible for the feeling that "our group is better than their group"[2] which supports the practice of excluding others.

This means that if you are with an intimate partner, you are designed to feel safe, even if your brain knows that this partner has hurt you. Threatening situations, even those created by your partner, may encourage you to return to a secure base and the strengthening of social bonds, which are, provided by your partner. So, a cycle ensues. You feel threatened and then you form a tighter bond with the person threatening you.

This triple whammy makes it very difficult for a person to be rational when they have pair bonded with an unfavourable person.

Simply put, they feel safer with this person and they feel separate from other groups of people. Even though significantly fewer people follow someone around all of the time, the bonding is just as strong and may be just as inappropriate as a duckling following a wolf.

In addition to oxytocin; opioids, norepinephrine, vasopressin and likely more hormones, all seem to play a role in attachment.[3] All of these hormones work together to ensure that humans bond with one another because "imprinting" is just as important in human social interactions and survival of the species as it is to the duckling.

Opioids are released during relationships and may be responsible for how awful we feel during a break up.[3] We become addicted to them, in the same way that we become addicted to taking drugs, and consequently feel the same withdrawal and the associated pain when the relationship ends.

It has been shown that some people with callous-unemotional traits[4] are not as affected by oxytocin. So, in a relationship with say, a narcissist, you get a hit of oxytocin and further bond and they may not have the same hormonal response, so they do not bond the same. This immediately tips the power into their favour.

All of this science is a way to emphasize that if we find ourselves in these terrible relationships, perhaps with a narcissist for instance, we should be gentle with ourselves. Our biology, in these cases, is working against our greater good, not unlike the duckling imprinting on a predator.

1. Journaling

Part of the power that the narcissist has is that they know that you cannot be completely sure of yourself and they occupy that space like ice freezing in a crack, expanding until a large hole is left where your confidence used to be. Journaling is the tool you need to protect yourself when they start to rewrite history or say things that make you question yourself. A record simply allows you to check your notes.

Particularly at work, or if dealing with a neighbour on an issue, it is important to make a record of any conversations that you have regarding anything controversial or anything that you are working on together. Take photographs, keep a log of events, and make sure that you are recording what is happening.

If the narcissist is in your social circle, keeping a record will help you figure out why there was drama, what went wrong. It also allows you to separate the facts, as you observed them from what you "heard" or were told.

Since narcissists often lie to make others look bad, you may be told that someone did something or said something, when in fact, you have no idea if this happened unless you saw it for yourself. Having a written account of what happened (even if there was no drama) is a powerful way to regain your sanity. Even if your recollection and the recollections of the narcissist differ, you will know for sure that you have a record of the way that you remember how things happened.

What is likely to bubble up in social situations is that when you analyze them, the person you thought was causing the discord, actually isn't. Some narcissists are so charismatic, that no one suspects that they are actually the one that is causing all of the disagreements and misunderstandings.

If you are in a more intimate relationship, one of a parent, child or lover, it is recommended that you start journaling regularly. The main reason that things need to be written down is so you will remember how bad you felt and what happened. Putting your experiences in writing brings them into a new light both literally and figuratively. When you reread painful passages written, by someone you absolutely trust (yourself), you see what happened in a completely new way.

Also, it is common to underestimate how awful something in the past felt. By promising yourself that you will never exaggerate, you can revisit how you actually felt. It will surprise you to see how differently you remember the bad times. An evening of tension is unpleasant at the time but the mind has a way of forgetting the bad parts of our lives. After a couple of weeks, you may only remember what you did and the bits that you enjoyed. It will be harder to tell yourself that it is not as bad as you imagine because you wrote down how you actually felt at the time.

If you are trying to bring sanity to a relationship with a narcissist that is a sibling, friend, co-worker or a parent, the journaling will help you see the relationship more clearly and "stand outside" of it. This will help you understand how to interact with these people (or not interact) in a less upsetting way.

If you leave a narcissist, that is your lover, while they are still pursuing you, they may try to get you back for a very long time. They do not like to "lose" and if you leave them it can be seen as you "winning" so they'll do everything that they can to dupe you into coming back. As I explained in the section on leaving the narcissist, becoming less valuable to them so that they replace you can help reduce the possibility of this, but it is not always possible.

When they try to "win" you back, the charming, solicitous version of their personality will show up. This is the imaginary one that does not last. It is very important that you have an accurate record of how you felt while you were still with the narcissist. Reread it before they arrive at your door. This will help you fortify yourself against these advances. Let's not forget, you may be lonely and going through the emotional turmoil of a break up when they try to win you back so you will be VERY vulnerable.

When you record in your journal, be as accurate and honest as you can possibly be. Do not exaggerate. If you feel really, really bad, you need to describe how you feel as well as you can. It is helpful to notice and describe how this pain and distress feels in your body. Try to describe how your body feels without using words that describe emotions. For instance, do not say, "I feel angry" to describe how your body feels, use words like pain, heat, tightness, tingles, knots or vibrations. It can be surprising how much we forget about the bad times. Journaling helps you to remember just how bad it got and by promising yourself that you will not exaggerate and that you write only true facts you can remind yourself of how things were.

Record the good times and the bad. Try to make notes about what preceded the bits that you like or did not like. The purpose of this is to see if there is a pattern. In a healthier relationship, nice time together is followed by a sort of after glow. You had a great day together and now you are content, perhaps at work or doing what you do in a day.

In a narcissistic relationship, time spent together is used as a way to meet the needs of the narcissist, whatever they are, and now you are not needed. There is no "after glow" you are now ignored. They may not have even spoken to you before you left the house. You have no idea what you have done to make them so distant. Fights may spring out of nowhere. Romance is always in pursuit of things. Keep as many notes as possible, because if you try to discuss these concerns with your partner they will deny the patterns, rewrite the sequence of how things happened and make it about you, not them. It is never their fault.

A journal can take many forms. It can be written on a computer, on pieces of paper or in an actual bound book, but it is important to write everything down.

Also, you need to have a private place to keep your journal. If you are working on a word document on a computer most of the programs will allow you to password protect your writing under the security setting. Blogs can be set up on the Internet. It is possible to configure them so that they are not public and it can all be kept private. These blogs can only be accessed through logging in and choose *"do not save"* the passwords in your browser. There is an option to *"never save"* the password for most browsers. Hard copies need either a private workspace at an office or in the home or a locked drawer or cabinet.

I am stressing this because if the narcissist knows that you are keeping a journal they will do everything in their power to read it. Once they have read it they will explode and this can put you in a very dangerous situation.

If you are no longer living with the narcissist, care should still be taken. Narcissists do not respect boundaries and may enter your home or ask someone who lives with you and trusts them to deliver the journal to them.

Absolute privacy is essential if you are going to be completely honest. When you are recording what has happened, and how you felt, it is imperative that you be able to write without censoring yourself. If there is a possibility that your work will be read, this is not possible.

Exercise 5   Journaling

Key Points on Journaling

Privacy
Write often
Record the facts
Do not exaggerate
Record what you think
Record how your body feels
Write in as much detail as possible
Reread your journal before seeing your narcissist
Reread your journal when you are at risk of returning to
the relationship

2. Releasing Emotions

Expressing emotions around a narcissist is a good way to become the target of their disgust, their anger or their taunting. Many of us who lived with a narcissist taught ourselves how to remain emotionally stoic as much as possible. Even laughter was ridiculed in my relationship. It was beneath the narcissist to laugh at something that juvenile or unexceptional.

The problem with emotions is that they must be released. If you do not actively express an emotion, the energy that is generated by the emotion has a way of staying in your body. When trapped in your body, these emotions can cause pain, discomfort and disease. Also, they are always trying to get out. So, if you are tired, stressed or upset all of the pent up emotion is just waiting for you to let your guard down and then you laugh hysterically when something was not that funny, burst into tears watching a commercial on television or snap at someone who did not deserve it.

Many of our addictive behaviours including alcohol, drugs, shopping, working excessively, eating, gambling and many, many more are a way to keep these emotions from being expressed. If you are trying not to "feel" an emotion that is trapped inside, you have to either keep busy or keep medicated.

The only way to release emotions is to allow yourself to feel them. Since it is often not appropriate to express emotions when they occur, you must set aside times for emotional release. I don't know why, but I can state for sure, that if you are trying to do this exercise while drinking alcohol it does not have the same healing benefits. I cannot speak to other forms of drugs but I have observed many, many people who cry and sob while drunk and are still very "full of unexpressed emotions" when they are sober. So, it is important that no alcohol be used before you do this exercise.

Exercise 6   Releasing Emotions

1. Find a time and a place that is as private as possible.

2. Pull a blanket or quilt around your shoulders and elicit any mood that surfaces.

A whole range of emotions can come up when you do this. If you know you are sad, for instance, you may play sad music or watch a movie that you know will make you cry. If you are angry, have something soft that you can pound on or some rags that you can tear. If you are lonely, have something to hold. You need to fall into the experience of the emotion and to just "let go" of trying to keep the emotion reigned in.

It is important during this exercise that you let the emotion happen.

This can be painful and may catch you off guard. Be prepared. Let it happen. Even if the experience is really painful, each wave never seems to last more than about 90 seconds, so you don't have to worry about falling into an emotion and never resurfacing. (There may be more than one wave during a session.)

It is normal to start with one emotion and have it morph into another one. You may start out as angry and then once you have raged for some time you might become sad or lonely. This is normal.

Do not try to talk to yourself about what is happening.

It is OK to feel something without trying to understand why you are feeling it. I used to tell myself, things like, "Yes, you are sad, but it is for the better". I was effectively jumping to the end without doing the work. By deciding that "It was for the better" I knew how I was 'supposed' to feel about the situation, which is quite different from allowing myself to feel whatever it was that I was feeling.

Also, another pattern is to get into telling yourself a story. "They shouldn't have done that". "I shouldn't have done that." "It should've been different." This is the "word generating part of your brain" trying to make sense of the emotion. Let these thoughts fall away and don't pay attention to them.

Focus on the sensations in your body.

Try to describe in words the way it feels when the energy of an emotion is being expressed. Fully engage yourself in the experience of feeling the emotion without trying to understand why it is there or what it means. If you cannot ignore the "word generating part of your brain" use descriptive words to describe how the emotion feels, if necessary.

These sessions can be very draining and it is important to do this when you have enough recovery time. For instance, you would not want to choose to do this when you are about to go to work, for instance. Afterwards, take the time to take care of yourself. Have a shower or bath, a walk outside in the fresh air, apply moisturizer, listen to uplifting music, watch a favourite program on television or write in your journal. Take the time to let yourself know that you are caring for yourself.

If a memory of an event elicits an emotion when you cannot express it, make note of the memory and revisit it when you have a chance to release the emotion associated with it. Do these sessions as often as possible. You will know that you are making progress when you start to feel more open to the beauty in the world.

3. Taking Care of Yourself

As you move away from the narcissistic relationship, you will have to rebuild a sense of who you are outside of the relationship. This can be a very difficult time because many of us were truly confused about who we were and what we wanted by the time we were able to free ourselves.

Read as much as you can about the condition. I have included a suggested reading list at the back of this book. It can be invaluable to recognize that you are not alone and to see the insights that other people have had about narcissists and the impacts that narcissists can have on your life.

Get outside as much as possible. Nature has a way of helping the healing process, perhaps by reminding us that we are part of something much larger than ourselves and way more complex than we understand.

Consider trusting again. I don't suggest you just trust the next person who comes into your life, but at least start to question whether or not trust is a bad thing. Many of us who have been the victims of a narcissist, start to question this very concept. There are other people better trained to guide you along this path, I'll just say, that you should be open to the fact that trust is a good thing.

This is a very tumultuous time and it is beneficial if you have some friends or family who can help you recover from this relationship. Try to reconnect with old friends or family members who you may not have seen recently. Also, try to get out and do things that you enjoy so that you have the opportunity to meet new people.

You might consider therapy, but make sure that the person you go to is experienced with narcissism. It is almost impossible to fathom that people can be as nasty as narcissists can be and the wrong therapist may not believe you and support your recovery.

Try to reconnect with who you are and what you like. It may have been a very long time since you were free to spend your time the way that you want to spend your time. It also may have been a while since you were rested enough and felt strong enough to have interests of your own.

Take at least fifteen minutes a day to do nothing but sit. What I am describing is mindfulness or meditation. There are several advantages to meditation. It forces you to do nothing for a while.

This is important because one of the ways that people avoid their feelings is by being very, very, busy.

Meditation, or mindfulness, has been shown to decrease stress, depression and illness. It has been shown to slow the aging process and it is key in helping to break bad habits such as smoking or gossiping. So, by setting aside fifteen minutes a day, you are not only helping yourself feel better, you can improve your life.

Exercise 7   Meditation or Mindfulness

1. Set aside fifteen minutes.

It is important to try to make this part of your daily routine. You need to do absolutely nothing except sit still. If you find it impossible to sit still for this long, you can do an active meditation. By this I mean that you can do this while walking, riding a bike, running or swimming or any other methodic activity that does not require you to pay attention to the activity.

This is not the time to say, "Wow!" I can combine it with my exercise routine, because if you do you will be focused on the exercise. I do not want you thinking about how far or fast you have gone. It is also important to find an activity that does not require you to pay attention to other people or traffic.

2. Become the observer, pay attention to:
- your surroundings
- the temperature
- sounds
- the lighting
- smells
- how the surface that you are touching feels
- your body
- your clothing

3. Explore what you are observing
- How does it feel?
- Is it soft, warm, scratchy?
- Do you have any sensations anywhere?

- Picture the sensations in your body.
- What colour are they?
- What shape are they?
- Do they have texture, weight or form?
- Is the appearance of them changing?
- Notice if there is any part of your body that is not relaxed. Relax it.
- Think about your breathing. Pay attention to the in and out movement of your breath.
- Can you hear your heartbeat?

4. Do not become engaged with the word generating part of your brain

During the time that you are meditating, there will be a part of your brain working on its own project. This is the word generating part of your brain and it will continue to generate words, even if you are trying to pay attention to the smells and sensations.

This is normal. Do your best to observe the words or to ignore them. Do not be drawn into what they are saying. For example, if the words you hear in your brain are you remembering that you forgot to go grocery shopping, don't start to make a shopping list. Be confident that you will remember to go shopping later and put your attention towards your toes, for instance.

I am not going to tell you that you have to stop that word generating part of your brain that has nothing better to do than jabber all day about this and that and all of the things that have happened to you. What you need to do is not pay attention to those thoughts, or said in a more positive way, pay attention to something else, like how your body feels.

When words come into your mind (and we both know they will) simply observe them and pay no further attention. It can be helpful to visualize them as bubbles that float to the surface and pop, or as cars speeding down a highway off into the distance, or any other visual that you may find useful. Do not criticize yourself for thinking, just notice and bring your attention back to your body or your breath or your surroundings.

4. Acceptance

I recognize that I outlined acceptance earlier in the book, but it is a very difficult process and it is worth discussing again. It does not mean that what happened is all right. It does not mean that you will forget. It means that it did happen and that is just a fact. No more and no less. It is actually quite important that you do not forget, because that puts you at risk of re-entering the relationship. You might want to refer back to Exercise 2 and 3 and review steps to help move this along.

Acceptance of what is.

This is not about what is good or bad, how this impacted your life, whether or not it should have happened. That is not what this is about. This is about the fact that it did happen. No amount of wishing, hoping or rewriting of history will change that. When you catch yourself saying things like, "If _____ hadn't happened, then _____ would be better today" you know that you still have work to do. If you still berate yourself for mistakes you have made or if you still think things like, "They shouldn't have done that!" You still have work to do.

It can be helpful to know that most people are doing the best that they can at any time. Yes, many narcissists seem to be purposefully hurting those around them, but we actually have no way of knowing if that is why they do it or not. We only know that they do it. A narcissist may be manipulating and hurting you, but this may simply be who they are. It does not make it right, it just makes it a fact. This is how they are. They are being true to themselves. This does not make what they do "acceptable" just a fact. It also does not make it less hurtful and I'm not suggesting that once you accept this you go back for more.

When you come to an understanding of a narcissist, their behaviour and their treatment of you, spending time with them is something that YOU are doing to yourself. You know how they behave. If you choose to spend time with them, you are the one causing the hurt that occurs.

There is an exception here for people who don't have a choice, or rather, the choice is to miss all family events or spend time with a narcissistic family member. A narcissist at work can also be impossible to avoid. But you need to get to a place where you either decide to stay and accept responsibility for how the relationship impacts you or you decide to leave.

2. De Dreu CKW, Greer LL, Handgraaf MJJ. Oxytocin promotes human ethnocentrism. Proc Natl Acad Sci USA. 2011 Jan;108(4);1262-1266. http://www.ncbi.nlm.nih.gov/pmc/articles/PMC3029708/
3. Nelson E E, Panksepp J. Brain Substrates of Infant–Mother Attachment: Contributions of Opioids, Oxytocin, and Norepinephrine. Neurosci Biobehav R. 1998 May;22(3):437–452.
http://www.sciencedirect.com/science/article/pii/S0149763497000523
4. Beitchman JH, Zai CC, Muir K, Berall L, Nowrouzi B, Choi E, Kennedy JL. Childhood aggression, callous-unemotional traits and oxytocin genes. Euro Child Adole Psy. 2012 Mar;21(3) 125-132. http://link.springer.com/article/10.1007/s00787-012-0240-6?no-access=true

Maintaining a Long Term Relationship

When I first start talking to people about the narcissists in their lives, one of the most common things I have found is that these people do not want to end the relationship, usually, they just want the person to start to behave in a way that doesn't hurt them. I am going to state clearly,

"The best predictor of future behaviour is past behaviour."

So, if you are in love with this person, or you love a parent, sibling or child that is a narcissist, you must begin there.

If you are choosing to maintain a long-term relationship with someone who is a narcissist be aware of how this relationship will impact your other relationships. If you are a parent, what are you teaching your children about self-respect and how to treat the people you love? How will this decision affect the other people who love you like your friends and your relatives? Will you be isolating yourself from your social circles? Are you choosing to stay because you have already alienated the other people who used to be in your life, or is it because you want to stay?

I must add in a word of caution here to those that are in intimate relationships. Narcissists have a way of eroding your self-confidence, undermining and sabotaging you and the longer you stay, the more damage they can do. During those periods when you are the receptacle, they may do things that will have a negative impact on your ability to earn money, your reputation, your credit rating and your health. They have the ability to interfere with your other relationships, alienate you from your family and strip you of all of your external support systems. This can lead you into a very dark place where you are at great risk of not recovering.

Can you love yourself and take care of yourself while part of this relationship?

The other groups of people who must maintain a long-term relationship are those that must stay in touch with a narcissist because they have joint-custody with a narcissist, their livelihood depends on it, the narcissist is the relative of a loved one and it is not their choice to end the relationship and a million other reasons.

The behaviour of a narcissist is not going to change. You must change how you interact with them so that you can decrease the negative impact they have on your life. There are rules that you can put in place to help with this.

1. Control Types of Contact

You need to set up acceptable times and ways that they can get in touch with you.

Some people set up specific email accounts that are only checked when it is convenient for the person receiving the email. There may have to be rules about whether or not they can call on the phone or in person and at what time and for what reasons. Be specific. If they do not follow the rules, the best thing is to just hang up. Don't forget, narcissists love drama, so if every time they call at one o'clock in the morning, you start to yell at them, that can be like candy. They are still managing to undermine you even though they don't live with you.

If it is OK for your employer or co-workers to contact you at home, there must be strict guidelines about how that is acceptable. They should not be showing up at your home or calling your private line unless you have consented to this.

2. Control Locations of Contact

It is important that there be specific guidelines about where they can meet you and call you.

It may be necessary to refuse to speak to them at work. To say that they cannot call you at work or come to where you work. This can be very important to keep their particular type of pathology away from your work place.

Employers and co-workers should only be contacting you through specific work channels and it must be clear whether or not you are expected to reply to emails and calls that occur during times when you are not working.

3. Demand Respectful Treatment

Be clear that they must be respectful in how they speak and what they say.

Some of the power of these individuals is that they can ruin your day by causing conflict, attacking you or undermining your self-confidence. It is within your rights to simply say, "I will only speak to you when you are using a respectful tone and being nice." This will not change them, but it gives you a way to walk away when they are not being respectful that does not have the drama of a fight that they so love.

It is never OK, even for your boss, to belittle you, personally attack you or make jokes at your expense. These are not acceptable and you should be clear about how you want to be treated.

4. Demand Advance Notice of Contact

It is responsible to require that you be told in advance when you will see them.

If you need to drop the children off, or if they need to pick them up, this can be at a set time. It is also useful to have another person stand in for these exchanges if possible.

You are not at the whim of their moods and if they want to see you, they can set that up in advance.

5. Set Personal Privacy Boundaries

Be clear about your boundaries, protect them with locks and passwords if necessary.

Make it clear that they are not to enter your home without your permission and that other people cannot invite them in. This must be discussed with all of the individuals that you live with.

If you are living with your narcissist, this may take the form of setting rules about your private space like a bedroom or office and when they are allowed to enter it.

In a work setting, it is reasonable to let your employer or co-worker know that it is unacceptable for them to enter your office without your permission. I would recommend locked drawers, passwords on email, computer access and voice mail if possible.

This set of rules will not protect you completely from the narcissist but it gives you more control over how their behaviour impacts your life. Setting these rules will not change how they behave, it just gives you some boundaries that you can use to manage the relationship. It also allows you to end contact, when it is inappropriate, in a way that is less likely to feed the drama that they crave.

Part 3: What Does This Mean?

Sorry, but this is the hard part. It is quite possible that your past relationships have had some residual impact in how you relate to your world. It is important to understand this so that you do not keep reintroducing the same pathology.

I begin by speaking to those of us that have chosen a best friend, or lover that is a narcissist and do my best to answer the question, "Why?". Then I talk more generally to everyone that may have had a significant relationship with a narcissist, even if it is a parent, sibling, relative or "significant influence" in your life. This influence may have been someone that lived with the family, dated one of your parents or in some other way became a large part of your life.

I begin with a look back at where many of us came from and talk about how these older relationships may have influenced us. Then I make some observations about what this might mean now. Finally, I wrap up the chapter with possible personality traits that you should be aware of in case you have adopted them.

Why Was I With a Narcissist?

So, after a terribly tumultuous time you have discovered that your partner is a narcissist. Yes, it is good to know that you are not going crazy. It is comforting to realize that you were not the source of all of the problems; you were simply the victim of a pathology masked as a lover. But, as the first wave of relief hits you, you begin to wonder, why did I pick a narcissist? This is a good question to ask, because it speaks to a deeper, often painful truth. A truth that you must understand before you pick another one.

Consider the following statements:

1. You had been lonely for a long time.
2. You are a gentle and open-minded person that is not quick to judge or jump to conclusions.
3. You are unable to distinguish the difference between someone who truly loves you and someone that pretends to love you.
4. You are highly independent and have learned to take care of yourself and those around you.
5. You knew that you could help this person achieve their full potential.
6. You thought that this person would make your life easier (more money, more support, more companionship).

Do any of these statements resonate with you? At first glance, the list above does not seem that remarkable. A lot of people are lonely. Being open-minded and self-sufficient are both good things. Knowing that you can help someone attain a better life, or hoping that someone can help you, both seem like reasonable things.

The alarming one is that you may be unable to distinguish between someone who truly loves you and someone who pretends to love you. When you combine that with one of the other things on the list, you can be exactly what the narcissist desires. Remember what the narcissist needs: the necessities of life, nourishment and a receptacle for their anger.

If you are willing to help this person achieve their full potential, or you are highly independent and can take care of yourself and those around you, the necessities of life may be what you can provide for the narcissist.

An individual that is looking for someone to take care of them, or is tired of being lonely is a sure bet for a narcissist. It is much more difficult for a person like this to leave an abusive relationship. Lonely or dependent individuals can swing between being a source of nourishment and a receptacle for the narcissist.

A gentle, open-minded person is easy to deceive. They are the type of individual that will give the narcissist "the benefit of the doubt" when the narcissist starts to show their true colours and this can lengthen the relationship considerably.

So these are some of the reasons that you may have been a target for the narcissist, but they do not speak to the larger problem, your ability to pick a partner might not be well developed. For many of us, we did not learn the basics of partner selection because we were brought up under less than ideal conditions. This is not to say that our families were not doing the best that they could, it just means that they were not equipped to help us to make good choices in the partner department.

> *You may have never*
> *experienced unconditional love.*

The fact that you chose a narcissist may mean that you have never received unconditional love. You may simply not know what this feels like. There can be many reasons for this. Your parents or guardians may have been narcissists themselves and were incapable of showing love. Your parents may not have been available to you because they were ill, too busy working or they had problems with addiction. True parental love differs significantly from conditional affection or kindness that is used to reward you for desired behaviour.

This means that you may have no basis for comparison. If you have never received unconditional love it is difficult to know how it feels or what to expect. In addition to that, the emphasis while I was growing up was always on "true love" as the gold standard for romantic relationships. This effervescent, transcendent thing was beyond definition except for the statement, "You'll know it when it happens".

More alarming than that was when I discovered that the true difference between lust and love, based on the above definition, was outcome. This is not a very good way to judge a relationship at the beginning. I am embarrassed to say that I may have tried to prove that I was in "love" not "lust" simply by staying in some of my relationships.

This "true love" view of the ultimate relationship is dangerous because it means that you are raised to believe that "love will conquer all" and that simply is not true, especially when the love is one-sided. Being raised with this notion of what love is plays right into the narcissist's hand.

The narcissist pretends to be deeply and truly in love with you. They need to see you all of the time. They may shower you with gifts. They want to spend every minute with you. They call, text, leave notes and basically reassure you constantly. They may also have this idealized "soul mate" vision that they convince you is attainable.

As I pointed out, while describing the signs that you are dating a narcissist, those behaviours are not actually love at all. This obsessive behaviour is smothering. Perhaps, not initially, but soon you realize that you cannot go out without disapproval. The narcissist needs to know where you are all of the time and there is no room for your wishes or desires.

So, lets look at what is important for the long term. The overall goal is being with this person enhances your life. They bring enough good that you are better off with them than you are without them. Sounds wonderful, but there are a lot of pitfalls in this, let me explain.

> *We all have needs.*
> *Needs to care for others,*
> *to be around others,*
> *to receive affection*
> *and*
> *to have companionship.*

If you have been lonely, like to have someone to take care of, or want to be taken care of, it may seem that the narcissist is "improving" your life simply by being around. The difference in a bad relationship is that spending time with them is often not that ideal.

Everyone has good and bad moods and cannot be expected to always be pleasant. The distinction with a narcissist is that they have extremes and they are unpredictable. This creates two problems. The first is that there is an uncertainty when you are with them about what type of mood they are in and what type of mood they'll be in soon. This puts a lot of pressure on you to 'behave' in a way that you know will lessen the possibility of them becoming unpleasant.

> *Narcissists have extremes in moods and they are unpredictable.*
> *Relationships with them differ in intensity with the*
> *"good being very good and the*
> *"bad being very bad".*

The second thing is that the swings are extreme. Some of the people that I have coached on this adore the *passion* that a narcissist brings to the table, but this enjoyment is usually short lived. What is happening is not the normal ups and downs of day-to-day life. It is the mood swings of someone that is not stable.

A narcissist will use extreme anger or self-pity to control a situation. "Poor me" no one loves me. Or the opposite, "Fine, I won't speak to you for days and days on end". Both of these responses are exaggerated.

In normal relationships, a partner may lose their temper, be snippy or mean and then immediately become remorseful because they realize that they have hurt you. The narcissist will not recognize that they have hurt you because they have an inability to empathize. You find yourself demanding an apology and whether or not you get it is not the point. You have discovered that this person did not "care" that they hurt you.

We need to examine
2
things at the beginning of any relationship:

1. Are they capable of love?

2. What is reasonable to expect when someone says they love you?

Lets examine how to tell the difference. There are three things that we need to consider when we are trying to answer the above questions.

1. How they act is more important than what they say.

It is easy for a narcissist to tell you what you want to hear, so let's look at how those types of statements actually look and if they are doing what they say.

They say they support you.

Support is not a verbal thing. If they are your partner, support means that they do part of the work, talk to someone on your behalf, do things that make it easier for you to get whatever it is done. They do not just say they support you; they do something to show it. In addition to that, they will express kindness and encouragement. If someone is providing support, the work is easier with them around.

Ask yourself if your partner is helping you or if they are emphasizing that you should be 'independent' and not so needy. Does their "support" actually mean "allow"?

They say that they respect you.

Someone that respects you honours your privacy, priorities, opinions and accomplishments. They do not use jokes to undermine your self-confidence. They do not belittle you or insult your friends.

Is it possible for you to have a different opinion from your partner or do they have to have the last word? Can they see the grey areas that allow you to disagree without being shamed or treated like you are in the wrong? It is not respectful if you are forced to see the world the same way that they see the world.

Try setting boundaries around your private time, interests and friends and see how they react. Do they respect your right to choose how you spend your time and with whom? Do they respect your right to have your own opinions and be independent from them? Do they like you as you are, or are you expected to look and behave in certain ways?

They say that they are your best friend.

Best friends are people that bring out the best in you, make you feel good about yourself and enjoy doing some of the same things that you do. They listen to you when you speak. They share excitement about your accomplishments, celebrate when you are happy and console you when you are upset. After spending time with a friend, you should feel good. Friends will try new activities with you. Does your partner rejoice when you share good news?

Observe whether or not your partner is a sore loser and has an unhealthy need to win or be right at all costs. Invite your potential partner to try something that you enjoy and that they have never tried. What type of reaction do you get? Do they go through the motions or do they actually get involved in the new activity to see if they like it?

They say that they love you.

When someone loves you, they love you all of the time, not just when they feel like it or when they want something. Even if they are mad at you, they do not put you down, insult you, attack you or undermine your self-confidence. If they do lose their temper they are immediately remorseful and will offer an apology. If a balanced person is angry with you they may not speak for a couple of hours, but giving you the silent treatment for extended periods, or often, is an attempt to control you. A person that loves you will not be trying to control you.

In a normal relationship, the affection ebbs and flows without attachment to what can be gained from the exchange. Sex and time spent together is followed by warmth and contentment, not abandonment and being ignored. You deserve love, attention and affection that you can depend on. If you are ignored or treated like an inconvenience, at any time, this person does not love you. How do they respond when you are sad, happy, concerned, late? Are they capable of showing love when you need it? Are they capable of showing empathy and understanding?

2. How they treat other people is how they will treat you.

How do they treat people that they don't know?

At a minimum, a nice person is courteous and may also be helpful when dealing with people that they encounter during the day. Does your partner show concern for other people? Or do they make jokes at other peoples' expense? Is their humour mean or based on how stupid, incapable or unattractive people are? Is it racist or sexist?

An honest person acts with integrity. Sometimes a narcissist will boast about being able to "pull one over" on someone. They will be just as dishonest with you.

What types of friends do they have?

It is important to meet your partner's friends. Normal people have friends that share the same interests, get together to do things they enjoy and support each other in good times, working times and bad times. Does your partner act differently around their friends? Behaving in a different way around friends is a red flag because it means that they are dishonest. Especially around friends, an individual should be comfortable relaxing and being themselves. A person capable of loving someone will be capable of forming strong bonds with good friends.

What types of dynamics are at play in their family?

Visit. See how they treat each other. Are they supportive and kind or are there a lot of mean jokes and put-downs? Is the mood festive, or subdued? Are the family members sharing stories and anecdotes? How are these stories received? Is there a feeling of openness and sharing or are one or two people asking a lot of questions?

Despite how family gatherings are stylized on television, many, many families actually enjoy each other's company. Is your partner kind to their family members or do they "hate" some of them? Are they "annoyed" by their families? A person capable of loving someone will show love and respect for their family.

How did their last relationship end?

An individual may have been hurt, disillusioned or abandoned by their last relationship, but it is important to ask detailed questions about what happened. A person capable of loving another will be able to explain in concrete terms what was wrong, how the relationship ended and why it didn't work. Claiming that their Ex was just "crazy" or "insane" is likely a major red flag.

3. How they express their emotions and feelings is important.

Balanced individuals express a range of emotions. They can be happy, sad, excited, angry and content. Is the full range of emotions expressed? Are you allowed to express the full range of emotions or are you told to "suck it up"? How does your partner respond when you need comforting, emotional support and attention? These should all be available when you need them. I do not mean that your partner should be available 100% of the time, but when you feel sad, for instance, they should recognize that you need comfort.

It is not unreasonable for you to want someone to spend time with you if you are in distress. There are limits to this; if you are distressed all of the time, but you should be able to rely on emotional support.

Is your partner open about their feelings? Have they managed to work through old painful memories or do they still find them overwhelming? Can they express the full range of emotions or do they mainly express the familiar narcissistic ones, which are: "poor me"; "I hate something" and "Wow! I'm great".

So, the final thing that you must face head-on is, "Are YOU capable of loving someone?" Do you feel empathy when someone else is being emotional or does it make you uncomfortable? Any relationship that you are in should be an equal partnership and if you are not capable of forming these bonds, you may not be capable of having a relationship with someone that can.

Traits You May have Picked up

We all have some of the characteristics of a narcissist, and even narcissists themselves are on a spectrum from the most extreme to having only a few of the characteristics. If you have spent time with a narcissist, or several, you may have picked up some of their traits. Dr. Karyl McBride has rewritten the diagnostic criteria so that you can ask yourself these questions:

1. "Do I exaggerate my accomplishments and say I have done things that I have not done? Do I act more important than others?
2. Am I unrealistic about my thoughts and desires regarding love, beauty, success, intelligence? Do I seek power in these things?
3. Do I believe that I am so special and unique that only the best institutions and the highest academic professionals could possibly understand me?
4. Do I need to be admired all the time to the point of excess?
5. Do I have a sense of entitlement and expect to be treated differently and with more status than others?
6. Do I exploit others to get what I want or need?
7. Do I lack empathy and therefore never see what others are feeling or needing? Can I put myself in other people's shoes? Can I show empathy?
8. Am I jealous and competitive with others or unreasonably, without logic, think that others are jealous of me?
9. Am I a haughty person who acts arrogant and 'better than' with my friend, colleagues, and family?

And I would add one more:
10. Am I capable of authentic Love?" [5]

Take a long hard look at this list. Discuss it with a close and trusted friend. Be honest with yourself and see if you have adopted any of the traits of a narcissist.

5. Karyl McBride, *Will I Ever Be Good Enough* (New York: FP Free Press, 2008) 218. http://ow.ly/28ipYM

Being in a pathological relationship is by definition, emotional abuse. The physical bruises and broken bones might not be present, but the wounds can still be deep and lasting. One of the ways that many of us survived was by learning behaviours that protected us, in some ways, from the abuse we were receiving. Taken out of context, as in when there is not a narcissist around, these can be maladaptive behaviours that can be misinterpreted by others.

Some people refer to these behaviours as "fleas". It is an apt metaphor because you can get them from other people and they are irritating, but you can remove them as well. They are not your normal way of behaving, just a way you learned to cope with your circumstances. These can be destructive behaviors that do not always shine the best light on you. Take a look at some of the examples below and see if they resonate with you.

> *You are not likely to have all of the traits, but you may have some.*

1. Appearing Emotionally Immature

Even if you are no longer in the abusive relationship and have sworn "no contact", some of the behaviours you learned to deal with the situation may have become patterns, so they are worth looking for. When you are with someone that has learned to manipulate you through making you feel bad about yourself, you become what I call, *"emotionally raw"*. Picture a skinned knee. Eventually, it will scab over and heal and the skin below will return to normal, but, right now it is fresh and bleeding. Any touching, even for cleaning, causes an immense amount of pain.

Your wounds are intentionally being kept open by your narcissist. That means that when you are with other people you might

overreact to slights

or

feel the need to defend bad behaviours

instead of taking responsibility for them.
You might also

strike out against people

using offensive or inappropriate remarks as a defense tactic when a normal comment would do. The other people don't know you're bleeding and hurt. They only see the extreme behaviour and it is difficult to comprehend why someone would behave that way.

Another thing that a narcissist will do is control, which emotions may or may not be expressed. This is done through criticism, taunting, attacks and the silent treatment. Some emotions are not allowed and you learn not to express them. If anger was acceptable and sadness was not,

you might appear hostile when you are actually hurt.

If only overly positive emotions were allowed and anger was not, you might appear to be

making fun of someone when you should be taking them seriously.

There are countless combinations of emotions that could have been either allowed or not allowed. There is also a possibility that what was acceptable would change and so you learned to not express any emotions. In any case, not being allowed to show a normal emotional reaction could result in what would appear to be an

inappropriate emotional reaction to a situation.

These responses would be incomprehensible to anyone that has not lived with a narcissist so it would make people think that you might not be normal, or worse that you are callous and uncaring.

You may have learned to hide emotions as much as possible. The problem with holding emotions at bay and not expressing them is that you need to let them out at some point. If you don't express your feelings when something happens, the emotions will build up and when your guard is down or when you get ticked off you will

have an exaggerated emotional response.

Overblown responses may take the form of anger, laughing, crying or any other emotion, and they may make you appear immature. Unfortunately, they can be expected from anyone that does not express their emotions especially when they are emotionally raw.

You may also not realize the appropriate way to behave when you see someone in pain or upset. Generally, people comfort each other. In a narcissistic household, someone that is upset may be ridiculed, coddled or ignored. Reflect back on your experience and observe how you react when you see someone in distress.

Are you able to show others that you care how they feel?

The opposite may be true. It is possible that only highly emotionally charged situations got attention. You may find that

you exaggerate how you are feeling.

This might take the form of being overly hurt or insulted. You may be overjoyed at the smallest event or amazed at something minor. This may have been one of the ways you could be "seen" in your home. Normal reactions may not have generated any interest.

In order to release the emotions that you have stored up you need to feel them. Allow yourself to experience your emotions as much as you can. I have explained this better in Exercise 6. Try to not pass judgment or tell yourself how you are "supposed" to feel or react. Relearning how to allow yourself to feel and express emotions is worth the effort. Try checking in frequently with your body until you understand how the sensations coming from it change. Meditation can help with this.

Exercise 8   Observing Emotions

a. Make a list of all of the different emotions you can name. Start with: mad, glad, sad or bad and then expand to include more specific ones like rage, joyful etc.

_____ _____ _____

_____ _____ _____

_____ _____ _____

_____ _____ _____

_____ _____ _____

_____ _____ _____

_____ _____ _____

_____ _____ _____

_____ _____ _____

b. Think of a situation with your narcissist present, if possible, when you felt each of these emotions.

> *i)*   Circle the emotions have you no memory of actually feeling.
> *ii)* Put a check mark beside the ones that you expressed.
> *iii)* How did the narcissist react?

c. Revisit this exercise as memories come up about particular situations. Having an actual record of how many emotions you feel, how you act and how you were treated is a good starting point to recognize how you respond now.

2. Refusing to Ask for Help

Since a narcissist never wants to be inconvenienced by you or your needs, any time you ask for help you will be turned down, unless they are about to ask you for a favour or are trying to get back on your good side. Also, instead of saying, "no", they attack and make it because "you are too needy", "you can't do anything yourself", "you are too demanding", "you aren't smart enough to figure it out on your own" or whatever insult they prefer. In other words, they use your personal vulnerabilities as a way of manipulating you into believing you shouldn't need help.

Love and attention are given in exchange for other things in a relationship with a narcissist. "If you don't make dinner, I won't even speak to you or acknowledge your presence". This may not be said out loud, but when you've experienced the silent treatment for extended periods of time, you learn to behave a certain way. Consciously or unconsciously you find yourself doing everything that you can to make them happy. This may have included refusing to ask for help.

It is common for a narcissist to accuse you of being selfish when in fact they are usually the more selfish one. This may create an imbalance with

you becoming increasingly selfless. Everyone else is more important than you are.

This is a more socially acceptable way to behave than the bursts of anger discussed above, but in extremes it is abnormal. Also,

it puts you at risk of choosing another narcissist.

If you are selfless already, you are perfect. In addition to this, a narcissist may say that they will do something and then not do it. The result of this is that you become increasingly reluctant to ask for help, even when you need it. Why risk the attack when you know that they are unlikely to help you? How can you rely on anyone? You may become aggressive towards those individuals that ask for help.

You may see people that ask for help as weak.

The opposite reaction is to

learn how to manipulate people into helping you.

Or you may find another person in your life to do what you need done and

use them the way a narcissist would.
You might become bossy and appear arrogant as a way to control others

behaviour. All of these responses would make you look like a narcissist as well, but they are simply maladaptive survival techniques.

You see people that do favours for others as weak.

The best way out of this is to keep a journal and write down each time you help someone or someone helps you. How do you manage to get things done? Make a note of what other people do for you and see if there is one or two that you "control" more than others. Force yourself to ask people for help. This is honest.

Everyone needs help. Choose people that are the most likely to help you. Examine whether or not the relationships that you have are reciprocal or if they are imbalanced. Observe this dynamic between you and your friends and family. What is your role?

Observe how you feel when you hear about someone else getting a favour. Do you think less of someone that asks for help? Why? It is normal for people to help each other. We live in societies because we need each other. We all need it and we all deserve it.

Exercise 9   Examining Beliefs

Take the time to think of two or three people that you know that ask for help a lot. Especially focus on people that receive the help.

a) What do you think of these people?

_____

_____

_____

_____

b) Why do you feel this way?

_____

_____

_____

_____

c) If you feel this about others how does it make you feel when you ask for help yourself?

_____

_____

_____

_____

3. Lack Self-Confidence

Part of the abuse you received while you were with a narcissist is that you were made to feel "less than." A preferred way to manipulate people is to make them feel that no one else would put up with them. No one would tolerate your (insert your own button here). The result of this is a profound loss of self-confidence.

When something did go wrong or an error was made, it was usually your fault, or blamed on a "scapegoat" in your household. Any conversation during which there was disagreement was used to assign blame and ensure that the narcissist was not at fault.

Arguments, or heated discussions were not about resolving issues they were about pointing fingers. Your response to this can take many forms.

You may be aggressive and arrogant as a way to cover your insecurity.

On the other hand, you may simply defer to everyone else's opinion,

seldom speaking up for yourself.

Either way, a calm confidence in your own opinion is not what you are expressing. If you were not on the defensive (which is caused by the narcissist) you could simply state what you think.

Any feedback would be seen for what it was; just a part of a conversation about a topic with different points of view and opinions being expressed. It is difficult to realize that people are not going to attack and blame you just because they disagree with you.

Observing yourself adamantly defend yourself, especially when you know you might be wrong,

is a warning sign that this is part of your unconscious behaviour. You may have also adapted to your situation by

acting more important than others

or

competing and trying to prove your worthiness.

"I am better than you are" or smarter, braver or whatever. You may find yourself exaggerating how wonderful you are. The opposite extreme is to compete for sympathy, "You may not feel well, but I feel awful." "You had a bad day, you should hear about mine!"

When you feel like you can't do anything right, it makes you more aware when other people make mistakes. A narcissist will use every error as more support for the hypothesis that you are not good enough. This makes you eager to point out other's mistakes. This can be seen as

intolerance for other's mistakes.

You make sure that everyone is aware when someone makes mistakes, which makes you look petty and vindictive, when in fact you are just insecure and trying to prove that you are no worse than anyone else.

4. Living a Fantasy

Narcissists lie. I know, I shouldn't just blurt it out like that, but it is true. One of the things that they use this skill for is to inflate whom they, what they've done and what they are likely to do in the future. This imaginary world that they create can be confusing because it is easy to think that they believe it...and they may.

If you live with this for a long time you might find that you have become accustomed to

looking down on others as inferior.

No one is as gifted, talented and deserving as you and your family. You may also have an inflated sense of your entitlement.

You may believe that you are the most successful, beautiful or intelligent.

Some of this may or may not be true, but you have been subjected to this fantasy creation for so long that it is even more difficult than average to be objective.

It is easy to get pulled into the illusion that is created with the web of lies. It can be very comforting to think that you

know more than anyone else

and that you are the only one that is "right". This extreme form of having an opinion and arguing it at all costs is simply a reflection of insecurity, not better information, greater intelligence or an ability to understand.

Everyone forms their own opinions based on the information that they have at hand and their own experience. Standing firm that any opinion is the "right" one and all other opinions are "wrong" feels strong but actually lacks wisdom.

It is very seductive to be with someone that is very confident about how right they are until you realize how foolish they actually look to others around them. It is not possible to know anything for sure. All you know is what your opinion is.

You may also have an inflated sense of entitlement and feel as though only the very best is good enough for you.

You may be insulted if you are not treated preferentially.

This, of course, stems from the fact that you were living in the narcissist's fantasy for a while and came to believe that some of the lies or exaggerations were true.

The opposite response to this situation is that you might

worry that people won't believe you or take you seriously.

You secretly fear that you are not as successful, intelligent, accomplished, *insert descriptor*, as the narcissist that you've been living with and therefore people will not think that you are valuable.

117

5. An Inability to Trust

The lies have another impact on your perception of the world around you. You may have developed an inability to trust. If you happened to be the receptacle of the narcissist; a term I use as the person that gets blamed for things, baited and undercut, you may also fear that people are out to get you. Or the "scapegoat" in a family of narcissists, someone HAS been out to get you, but behaving like this is still happening can have a negative on your relationships.

If you interpret every mistake as a slight and proof that

people are out to get you,

you are still in pain from being undermined in your relationship.

Most people are not out to get you. Mistakes happen. They are normal and human. Being paranoid is not ridiculous when you have been living with someone that is out to get you and to make you feel inadequate, small and 'less than'. But it does look bad when you interpret accidents as attacks.

The extensive lying leaves you less likely to be able to trust.

The inability to trust may superficially sound like a good thing. You may tell yourself destructive things like, "if I hadn't been so gullible, I would not have believed everything". Deciding not to trust can feel like the perfect way to protect yourself, but ironically, it makes you more likely to end up with another narcissist in your life.

> *By not trusting you are effectively eliminating the potential friends and lovers that you actually want in your life and giving the narcissists the advantage.*

In order to form a genuine relationship with a new friend or lover, you need to be able to trust them, until you have a reason not to. At the beginning of a relationship there is always an exchange of information, favours and gestures. I'm not suggesting that you reveal highly personal information, but there is always a give and take while getting to know someone.

If you immediately distrust people, this exchange does not occur and the other person will likely decide that they don't like you, or were unable to get to know you or that you were not interested in getting to know them. Most people will not continue to try to get to know you, at this point.

The narcissist, on the other hand, will start to flood you with assurances. They will call repeatedly and let you know that they think that you are wonderful and the centre of the universe (see Signs that You are Dating a Narcissist). They are the ones willing to go the extra distance to pursue you. Effectively, your inability to trust weeds out the people that you want in your life and selects for the narcissists.

Trust is developed over time, but assuming that you shouldn't trust someone right away sends out the wrong message when you are first getting to know someone. Start slow, share "safe" information (that you would be Ok with everyone at work knowing) and make sure the sharing is reciprocal.

Since you are not going full speed into this relationship and spending every minute with this person, you have time to ask others about them (not just one person's opinion!! There is always a good chance that your confidant is a narcissist.) Meet their friends early in the relationship. Ask them to do things that you want to do. Have your friends meet them. Go out a lot without them, especially at the beginning. These are all ways to see if you should invest more in a potential friend or lover.

I'm not suggesting you blindly trust the next potential friend or lover, but I am suggesting that you give the person a chance to get to know you, and you them, before you decide not to risk it. As I've said before, the barriers we all put up weed out the good not the bad.

6. Depression, Anxiety, Nervousness

Finally, you probably experienced emotional hardship at the hands of your narcissist. This could leave you

depressed, "emotionally raw", anxious, nervous, sad, angry.....

There are as many possible emotional responses as there are people. Be honest with how you are feeling. Honour your experience. Try to observe how it is affecting your behaviour.

You may have turned to addiction.

This could be legal or illegal drugs, eating, working, shopping, sex, gambling etc. These are all a way of not confronting how you feel. They keep you numb or preoccupied so that you don't feel all of the emotions that are waiting to come out.

Know there is a hole in your heart and a tear in your self-confidence that need mending. The work required takes a lot of time and support and it is a painful process, but it is worth it. Becoming aware of how this experience may have changed how you act is a good step forward and away from that part of your life.

Reread Exercise 6 and try to allow yourself to feel the emotions that are trapped. Allow all of your emotions to surface.

Recognize that there are hormones that keep you bonded to people and if you are trying to go no contact with parents, siblings or especially a lover, it will feel like you are withdrawing from a drug addiction. Get support.

The bad news is that these behaviours can make you look like a narcissist. The good news is that you are not and the behaviours can be unlearned. Once you recognize that you have behaviours that you would prefer to not have, it is just a matter of paying attention and learning to react, or not react, a different way.

Knowing as much as possible about what is actually happening to you and around you is very helpful as you start to heal from the trauma of having a narcissist in your life. The simple fact that you were not insane, you were not unlovable or selfish, you were being emotionally abused is enough to help regain a part of what you lost. It is possible to move through the emotions, learn about the pathology and emerge into a wonderful life.

It is a life-long process to move through the pain and work towards bringing more joy and authenticity into your life. You never truly "get over" some of the more serious aspects of having a narcissist in your life -- especially if this person was very close to you -- but you are capable of healing and finding life after the narcissist.

Now that you have some tools to identify these individuals, deal with the ones that are in your life, you are well on your way to reclaiming a life that you love. Take care of yourself and good luck on your journey.

Suggested Reading

Will I Ever Be Good Enough?: Healing the Daughters of Narcissistic Mothers
This is an insightful book written for those of us who had a parent that was a narcissist.

http://ow.ly/28ipYM

The Sociopath Next Door
This book is an insightful piece about how to identify a sociopath and protect yourself.

http://ow.ly/28iq6c

Disarming the Narcissist: Surviving and Thriving with the Self-Absorbed
This book gives information on how to spot a narcissist. Falls short in good advice about how to actually deal with one.

http://ow.ly/28iqeb

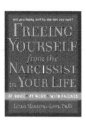

Freeing Yourself From the Narcissist in Your Life

Good description of what a narcissist really is.
CAUTION: Makes narcissists seem like heroes through the examples.

http://ow.ly/28iqs0

*Some of the links provided are affiliate links that generate a small commission.